The Road and the Miles

A Homage to Dundee

Other titles by Jim Crumley

Among Islands
Among Mountains
Badgers on the Highland Edge
Discovering the Pentland Hills
*Glencoe – Monarch of Glens**
The Heart of Mull
A High and Lonely Place
*Portrait of Edinburgh**
Royal Mile
*St Kilda**
*Shetland – Land of the Ocean**
Waters of the Wild Swan
*West Highland Landscape**

* with photographer Colin Baxter

The Road and the Miles

A Homage to Dundee

JIM CRUMLEY

MAINSTREAM
PUBLISHING

EDINBURGH AND LONDON

Copyright © Jim Crumley, 1996
All rights reserved

The moral right of the author has been asserted

First published in Great Britain in 1996 by
MAINSTREAM PUBLISHING COMPANY (EDINBURGH) LTD
7 Albany Street
Edinburgh EH1 3UG

ISBN 1 85158 787 X

No part of this book may be reproduced or transmitted in any
form or by any means without written permission from the
publisher, except by a reviewer who wishes to quote brief
passages in connection with a review written for insertion
in a magazine, newspaper or broadcast

A catalogue record for this book is available from the
British Library

Subsidised by

THE SCOTTISH **ARTS** COUNCIL

Typeset in Garamond by Blackpool Typesetting Services Ltd
Printed and bound in Great Britain by Butler & Tanner Ltd, Frome

To Vic and Sheenagh

Contents

Acknowledgments

The author would like to thank the people of Dundee, both living and dead, many of whom – knowingly and unknowingly – contributed wit and wisdom to these pages.

City archivist Iain Flett and Tayside Region planning director Jack Searle were particularly helpful and patient. Irene Rowe and Angela Mathers at *The Courier* were both kind and enthusiastic. And finally, my thanks to the Scottish Arts Council for a travel and research grant which greatly assisted my labours.

Chapter One

The Colour of Mud

There are few enough not born to the place who think of it as bonnie. That apparently bizarre coupling of words, 'Bonnie Dundee', may have gone into the language of Scots, but to legions of unbelievers it means either a page in the Corries songbook or the ultimate cliché of civic self-deception.

Bonnie Dundee was a man, of course, not a city. John Graham of Claverhouse, Viscount Dundee, and sometime of Mains Castle to the north of the city, was a charismatic Jacobite who was felled by a stray musketball at Killiecrankie in 1687 and in his hour of glory at that – all of which was excuse enough for Scotland to write a song about him. And no matter that he was also known among his contemporaries as 'Bloody Clavers', posterity cares to remember him as Bonnie Dundee. So why should not the city from which he loftily borrowed his own title loftily borrow it back?

There are those, of course, who will tell you that Dundee, the city, has not been bonnie for some time, a thousand years, say, since folk started heaping the local stone into narrow wind-cheating streets and away from the long-lost castle which began it all. That stone is the problem in any aesthetic assessment of Dundee. It is the colour of mud. When it has grown old and industrially grimy it is the colour of

11

new mud. Now that it has been much cleaned and rejuvenated, it is the colour of old mud. In Edinburgh, a low winter sun extracts flavours of honey in its Craigleith sandstone, and Aberdeen granite glitters like a starry night. In Dundee, the same light achieves a half-baked biscuit. It is a shade destined to be drab.

I was born to it on 6 July 1947, in an era when it was probably at its drabbest, and I have loved the colour of mud ever since.

This, then, is my homage to my native city. It is the city as I know it, not a history, assuredly not a guidebook, but a highly personalised and wholeheartedly subjective harvesting of thoughts and sentiments and (I hope) insights into a much misunderstood city, both in its benevolent midst and at enchanted distances. It is a city on which my family has left small imprints, and which has left one vividly indelible imprint on my family. To a man, woman and child, we still call it bonnie. And whenever I feel cold or wounded in the world beyond the Tay, Dundee is the hearth to which I return to warm myself and heal.

It is also a homage to Alfie.

I am not at all sure I can explain Alfie's presence in this book. I should have been able to write it without involving him. Yet he attends (in the manner of an attentive, hovering waiter, anxious not so much to be of service as to be conspicuously involved) on every pencil stroke, every deft expulsion by the pencil's rubber-tipped other end, every tapped typewriter key.

He is all the Dundee I have ever known which I didn't unearth for myself. He informs my thinking on the subject (mostly) subconsciously. He would not presume to edit me, nor to shape so much as a phrase. Yet were it not for his myriad interventions in that part of my life which remains locked inside the old mud-coloured walls, would I ever have written anything at all – this book or any other? Is he not, for better or worse, the sculptor of my native awareness, the shaper of my clay?

He is the untotalled sum of many of my life's parts, as blameworthy as he is creditworthy. He is mostly older than I am but not always. He is the perambulating spirit of that Dundee I grew up with, and he is bisexual.

What I mean by that is . . . he is a figment, an amalgam, a notional companion, a compendium of Dundee characters and characteristics:

the men and the women, the boys and the girls, the mates and the girlfriends, my parents and grandparents and their friends, the walk-on regiment of part-time relatives, neighbours, teachers, scaffies, rent men, coalmen, lemonade men, ice-cream men, shopkeepers, bus drivers and conductors, doctors, ministers, footballers, cricketers, newspaper sellers and newspaper makers whose paths have crossed mine.

So, he bides in meh heid, as he would say 'eesel, for he is as bilingual as he is bisexual. And why Alfie, and not Eck or Izzy or Annie, I have no idea. I know no one called Alfie and he has no clear face, but he is fair-haired, a touch overweight and invariably smaller than my all-but-six-feet. And tough, tough as Clydesdales and with just as big a heart. He is dirt-under-the-fingernails Dundee, probably the Hawkhill which he would call 'The Hahky', and intellectually impressive within the limitations which fate dished out to him, a world traveller by way of the 'lehbray'. He was born up a closie, he never lived anywhere but here, and if he went abroad at all, it was between the years of 1939–45. He thinks the sun rises and sets on Dundee, hates what 'they' have done to it, and won't hear a word against it. He laments passionately the demise of the Fifies and the Overgate, so he hates the 1960s; he gave the Beatles six months. He supports Dundee Football Club but is not averse to lending Dundee United his terracing lungs if he deems, on certain selected occasions, that they are carrying the honour of the city. He likes Jimmy Shand, Django Rheinhardt, Lester Young, Beethoven and Michael Marra. It is just possible that he worked in the last of 'the muhlls' or the shipyards; more likely he was a printer or a baker or a telephone engineer. He loves Saturdays and bairns and the smell of the sea and the kind of crack his father's generation was good at. So he dipped a toe at least into the waters of Dundee's continuity. And thus he is in a position to bridge the great breaches in that continuity for which 'they' are to be eternally damned and, by way of his bridge, folk like me can cross and look safely back to where we come from. Alfie.

I invented him thoughtlessly. I wrote the first line of a rough draft of what is now Chapter Two, and having written that line, frowned and asked my writing desk aloud: 'Who the hell is Alfie?' The desk was never built which was up to answering such questions, but he became better defined as I began the long solitary trawl through old haunts and old familiarities, sifting the chaff of a life for some ripened wheat. Alfie is the voice through which my home town speaks back to me.

He is also my navigator, charting routes through streets and prodding me down lanes, shoving me through doors into the walled garden of memory where a whiff of one more scent put ideas between my ears and words in my pen. And because he is a composite, I would meet him on every other corner where a snatch of conversation or a glimpse of a face I could put a dozen names to, a pretty passing face recalling a classroom crush, or some other gesture quintessential to this place . . . all of these would catch my eye, and my mind's eye would reorder them into that psyche of Alfie I had invented to be the embodiment of all of them.

The boy who became a man here also became a writer. It is as much a writer's eye which beholds Dundee now as a native's, and because of that it is as much inclined to take liberties as it is to observe and remember. So while there is fragmented autobiography of a kind here, there is also fiction, stories founded on scraps of Dundee circumstances which have intrigued me all my life. But there is purpose to these too, the purpose of shedding a little extra illumination under the skin of the mud-coloured stone.

For that mud shade is also a mask. It is apt to confound strangers, even repel them, to blind their eyes to the charms of a city which is as underrated as it is misunderstood. It is fair to say that it has not assisted its own cause by a crude disregard for its built environment through the 1960s, '70s and '80s. It has suffered, too, in that its former fame and prosperities were built on the back of a species of industrial sea-going which is now extinct. That extinction left a vacuum in which only purposelessness can thrive.

But Dundee people are stoics. We possess a calm self-containment and, when others wince at our mud-coloured walls, we draw a distinctive shade of comfort from them. And slowly, through the grey years, we have reassembled our self-belief, dusted down and shone up the ahld trumpet, and begun to blah it again. We have new songs to sing, and even if the new singers occasionally sound like a literal translation of the mud-coloured walls into music – which is how I fondly listen to Michael Marra, for example – we're calling our own tune again, and it may be that the rest of the country is, as usual, just a little slow in tuning in to its accent.

Alfie and I were in a convivial howff ae Se'erday where the said Michael was performing. A stranger at the next table was overheard by Alfie:

'I can't see what all the fuss is about. The man can't sing.'

'Eh, right enough,' said Alfie, 'jist like Louis Armstrong couldnae sing.'

Chapter Two

The Hully

'Why is Dundee,' asked Alfie, 'like a catamaran?' I thought about it for a moment. Alfie is a great one for puns, cueing them up from a great distance through a conversation. This one was the fag-end of a long discourse on Dundee's seagoing history – the whalers, the jute ships, Arctic explorers, lightships, lifeboats, coasters and ferries to Fife and, apparently, catamarans.

I'm not the most seasoned of seafarers – a voyage to St Kilda once, and a furrower of the Minch, and the North Sea as far as Shetland, and an addictive hopper-over to Skye and other Hebrides – but I've had Alfie skipper me through enough convivial evenings at the Ship Inn not to recognise that the tremendousness of his unassuming knowledge had lobbed in a wee squeeb a few minutes back, and I had waited for it to go off ever since. I glared at his eyes but his pan was as dead as ever. No clues there.

Catamarans . . . they're built on twa hulls, right? And Dundee is built . . . got it! . . . small smirk of triumph! 'Cos Dundee's built on twa hulls!'

Alfie's deadpan resurrected into half a grin and went havering off out to sea again.

Twa hulls. The language of meh ahld hame toon is both its own inimitable speech (rich in glo'al stops and gu'uralls, a tricky mélange of lowland Scots and a species of English curdled by violated vowels as broad as the Tay estuary) and a source of jokes at its own expense. It turns the science of phonetics on its arse, which is the best place for it. A simple word like 'I' becomes 'Eh', as in wet, but not quite – you need to rough up the vowel a bit; aye, as in yes, is also 'eh'; more famously, 'pie' has become 'peh' and a Dundee cliché. Among the many other improvements on English, 'hill' becomes 'hull'. So, Dundee is like a catamaran, built on twa hulls, and you have been wahrned: wahtch oo' fur squeebs.

The city spills down in every direction from the flanks of two hills, the Law and the Balgay, the Lah and the Hully. (Oh, oh, this may need explaining, too. The '–y' syllable gets stitched on to all manner of things and places, often after they have already been contracted in the first place. It serves no purpose whatsoever other than to endow a sense of intimate acquaintance; or maybe to confound strangers. Some examples are relatively easy – the Perth Road is the Perthy, the Blackness Road is the Blahcky; the Hawkhill is trickier because it becomes the Hahky; but the masterpiece was turning Constitution Road into the Conshy, and if you ever have cause to cycle up it, it's a right conshy and no mistake.) Back to the twa hulls. The Lah is higher and the more famous, the centrepiece. But the Hully's mine.

The Hully is where I come from. It is half woodland and half cemetery and, as my parents and three of my grandparents lie there, it may well be where I end up, regressing back into the soil, feeding worms for the blahckies to scoff – that's the other kind of blahcky, wi weengs. In the worm-scoffing, the blahckies will neatly conclude a satisfactory cycle of revenge. For the Hully was one of two doorstep domains of childhood (the other being the farm across the road – I lived in the Glammy when it was the last street in town) where nature and I first rubbed shoulders, and because it was what boys did then, we collected birds' eggs.

Collected – ha! All the nests I knew (we found our own and guarded them jealously) were blahcky nests. My collection at its peak comprised five blahcky eggs in a Milk Tray box stuffed with cotton wool, and one chaffinch egg which I had swapped for a sixth blahcky.

I was, you might say, the Hully blahcky eggy laddie. I never did become much of a collector of eggs or anything else, but even now, every orange-rimmed blahcky-black eye levels an accusation at me and I sense that one day there must be a reckoning. From the blahck-ies' point of view, if there is any natural justice, it will be seen to be done on the Hully. Fair enough. If that is how it all pans out, I shall have no complaint. For although there are more beautiful hills and shores which have seduced my turned back away from Dundee, here is the one place where my own characteristic restlessness likes best to draw breath, and knows it can be briefly still. Here I think only of where I stand; and quietly, I celebrate.

Mostly, too, I think back. The Horlicks of nostalgia is part of it all, but I have no problem with nostalgia when it is both grateful and respectful. Here is a wooded hill above a wide and handsome firth, a dark and perpetual crouch which wreathed my childhood in benevo-lent shadows and sheltered it from ill winds. I think of it often from those twin distances of miles and time, and if nostalgia has filtered out the memory of a few bruises, there were only ever a few in the first place and none caused lasting pain. I remember only happy times.

I fingered the word 'idyllic' here, but decided against it. This was, after all, post-war, pared-to-the-bone, corporation-prefab Dundee and there are glimpses of ration books in the darkest recesses of my memory. There were no idylls, not here, not then. Yet I only con-templated the word in the first place because it seems to me to have been as ideal a childhood as my kind of child could have desired. It revolved around the joys of an admittedly simpler time – football, cricket, bikes, food, the countryside which still lapped the far side of the street then, rising and falling over northbound contours to the summer-blue, winter-white northern bulwark of the Seedlies. (This is another choice example of the Dundee vocabulary: maps insist on misrepresenting and mis-spelling them as the Sidlaw Hills.)

The obvious omission from that list is the still centre of my young world – a three-room prefab and the parents who made it welcoming and metaphorically warm (in truth it was a winter ice-box) and estab-lished the values which prevailed upon my brother, Vic, and me. The prefab was designed by a genius, built to house homecoming war ser-vicemen and their families. They were supposed to stand for ten years. Ours stood for thirty and cradled the first thirteen years of my life.

The kitchen had a table and an ironing-board which folded into the wall, a gas cooker, a boiler and an immersion heater. The living-room fire had doors. The two bedrooms had built-in wardrobes and a dirty linen bin you could climb into. The bathroom and WC were separate. All this was achieved in a corrugated off-white box of almost bothy proportions. Its simplicity set the tone of our survival there. I suppose now that we were poor then. But our parents belonged to that war-coloured generation who could make shillings do the job of pounds, and we lacked nothing obvious. The prefab smelled of breakfast porridge, lunchtime stews (lunch was called dinner and dinner in the evening was a concept I didn't comprehend), afternoon baking, evening coal fires and the paraffin stove in the lobby. Summers we lived as much outside it as inside. I think we were all homesick for it forever, beginning on the day we moved out.

The prefab has gone. The farm across the road has gone. Suburbs reign far out into what we used to call 'Angus'. Skylarks have metamorphosed into pigeons. Nature has retreated west and north. But the Hully endures. And forbye the nostalgia there is this.

Landscapes are fundamental to what my life has become, the raw material for much of my work, the moulds which fashion my peaces of mind. Dundee folk are lucky. Ours is a city with both a landscape setting of rare distinction and an internal landscape. Often in these past years I have wondered about the germ of this passion-in-landscape which has flourished in me unbidden, egging me on beyond the strictures of journalism to writing adventures in such as St Kilda, Shetland, Skye, the Cairngorms, Iceland even. Here, amid the Hully's shadows, is the seedbed.

Landscape is the other force which draws me back. My father grew phlox and lupins here and I grew a mindful of landscapes. If your mind's eye is up to the task of paring away a few surface layers of civilisation's artefacts, here is no meagre landscape. Before nostalgia was invented, before the new suburbs, before the prefab, before the farm, before the cemetery . . . before all that, there was only a low wooded hill on a seaman's skyline, and from its modest summit a forty-mile-wide swathe of river and firth and open sea was your spreadeagled inheritance. The same modest summit instils in me an indefinable sense of well-being. It is more than nostalgia. I am rooted here.

The prefab stood on the north slope of the Hully in its winter shadow. When I was 13 we moved to a new flat on the east slope facing the Lah, the city and the sea. At 20, part of me left Dundee, hell-bent on journalistic glory, more or less as my parents finally cast adrift of the Hully (the hill and the four flights of stairs had become a wearisome pech) for a new flat in Broughty Ferry amid gull clamour and salt winds, and where, for the price of a short walk, you stood on a shore of the Tay more sea than river and seals eyed you from low-tide sandbanks and eiders and curlews crooned near your passing feet, and the Hully was far off and unfamiliar; a low wooded hill on a seaman's skyline again.

So home became the Ferry. But after eight years there my father died, and we trudged sorrowfully back across the city and laid him on a river-facing slope of the Hully, no more than a quarter of a mile from where the prefab had stood. It was October, the Hully was in its autumn shades. Faither was twenty years too soon and suffered too much in the going, but these huge considerations apart, he might have approved and admired the setting and the day.

THE BONNIE HULLS (by my father's grave)
A living man upon a deid man thinks
And ony sma'er thocht's impossible
> —Hugh MacDiarmid

'The Bonnie Hulls' – that sigh
was ever on your lips, your eye
on Tay's far shore, the Dreish
or Mayar, but here
on Balgay's modest brow
we made you hillside.

Earth-to-earth's fate fit enough
but I'll have no dust-to-dust here.
You leave a burnished legacy
I'll shine and shine dust-free
until I see your face in it.
I cast your eyes

On Tay's far shore again
and wonder whatna hulls
and rivers you've seen since
and in whas lugs
you cried them bonnie.

Eighteen years later, my brother and I buried our mother in the same grave. To walk the Hully now, is to reach back, and to acknowledge the source of a great earth-stillness beneath my feet which has become a constant and elemental companion. A vital stillness on which I have come to depend; an antidote to the restlessness I took away with me.

So that is where I come from. If you are inclined to test the woody embrace of the Hully, try a late afternoon of grey midwinter, snow and geese on the air, and have a pulse of yellow-white sun bounce up to you off the wide river scoop of Invergowrie Bay. That light flares against the sheen of the gravestones and blinds your eye to the names and remembrances on the stones. The deid, relieved at last of having to go on being who they've been, relax and go about their spiritual business commuting to their heaven on the wings not of angels but wild geese. If the winter waters of Invergowrie Bay don't correspond to your definition of heaven, you're just not long enough deid yet.

Or as Alfie told it in the Jeemy Shand ae nicht:

'Thur's these twa wifies up the Hully. Ane says tae the ither:

' "Ina! Whu ur you daen up here?" "Aw, Maisie . . . meh man's deid."

' "Ahld Spud? Deid? Awa tae hell!"

'"Eh?"'

A WHEEN O GEESE

A skein o westerin geese
— a wheen o whifflin weengs —
prowls aboot meh heid the nicht,
a featherweight ball and chain
that harks me back,
gaslit Dundee ablow
their frosty sing-songs, lullabeh
as soothing as Winnie-the-Pooh
or Horlicks. Fifies ferried
dreams to Newport then
and Dundee's thumpin heart
was stane.

But far from then and there
— on Flanders Moss the nicht —
the ring aroond the moon
ignites a wheen o geese
and in meh hamesick heid
it reconvenes the Hully's peace.

23

Chapter Three

The Tap o the Lah

The unbroken slopes of the twa hulls, the Lah and the Hully, collide in the trough of Lochee. The slopes are much built upon, of course, and much smoothed over, but if you could go back far enough you would find the east slope of one and the west slope of the other hinged together by a shallow sweet-watered valley, and Logie Street, Lochee, is the bed of its burn. On your way down the Hully, going east, the Lah rears compellingly. It becomes all the city there is, blunt and broad-shouldered crowned by its carbuncle of a war memorial. The hill is frizzy with trees now, like a cat that's been in a fight. I have not accustomed myself to those upstart trees. It was always the barest of hills. Old photographs, drawings, paintings and book illustrations are proof: it was long the barest of hills. My back was turned when the planting was done. I turned up after a twelve-month absence and found the deed done, the Lah bearded. I felt unconsulted.

The Lah is a volcano, its crater caved in and healed. The flat top it made for itself is handy for huge war memorials and car parks, and for walking about in a cooler, more exotic air than the city streets know about. You can pech up or you can drehv up. If you drehv, the road signs say 'Dundee Law' which is the one thing no Dundee voice ever cried it. Alfie is apt to call it 'The Lah Hull'. When you point out to him, tactfully uv coorse, that 'Law' is just a Scots word meaning 'hill' (**law** [la; Ne also lja] n. a rounded usu conical hill, freq isolated or conspicuous – *The Concise Scots Dictionary* to be precise, Alfie, ken?) so he's calling it the Hill Hill, he shrugs, faintly miffed:

'It's worth twa o any ither hulls Eh've heard o, so the Lah Hull's fine beh me, Jimmy. And if ye care tae stuff yer dictionary up yer concise Scots bumbeleerie (**bumbeleerie** la; Ddee, esp Hahky, bumbul-i-ri n. a rounded *usu* conspicuous feature of the lower rear aspect of the human anatomy, the source of shite – Alfie's Dad's Concise But Mostly Unprintable Scots Dictionary, Vol. 1 A–F, Jimmy, ken?) that's fine beh me'n'ah.'

It's the linguist in the man I'm drawn to.

The 'Dundee Law' signs flexed Alfie's imagination.

'It sounds like the title o a western.' He switched on a Hollywood drawl: 'John Wayne is Rooster Dundee. His law is Dundee Law.' And he cocked two threatening forefingers and thumbs at them from his waist.

'Or . . . it's a state o emergency, eh?' He switched on a po-faced Home Service voice: 'A state of Dundee Law has been declared throughout the land.'

We had, it should be explained, wetted wur whustles in the Anky. (Anky. Another malleation of the language. Anything to do with Ancrum Road is the 'Anky'. Ancrum Road Primary School, where I toiled seven years the only education I wholeheartedly enjoyed, is the Anky. But so – and this is the case in point – is the Ancrum Arms in Lochee.) So, after the whustle-wetting, we wandled warslin up the precipitous streets that are the reclaimed flanks of the Lah Hull, good-humoured from the Anky's charms and from the still, August blaze of heat that lay like a suit of armour on the whole city. We were, perhaps a little drunk from the sun-surfeit (an uncanny unbroken month, Dundee's climate rendered as benign as California's, sort of), and we embarked on a thoughtful cronie-ish surmise about the implications for society as a whole if a state of Dundee Law were to be imposed. 'So what would be the single greatest benefit fur wur fellae Scots under Dundee Law, Alfie?' I spiered.

Alfie paused in mid-stride, grasped a garden railing and a fistful of privet for buoyancy. He struck an imposing philosophical pose complete with a noble puckering of his brow.

'The single greatest benefit,' he began studiously, and paused again, 'wi'oo question,' . . . he stalled and paused again . . . 'ud be . . . ' he prevaricated. Surely, I urged, there *would* be a benefit?

Then, the spontaneous combustion of his facial expression:

' . . . Ud be – ahbdy'd tae acknowledge the superiority uv Wahlusses pehs . . . that's it! Wahlusses pehs on ahbdy's plates, and . . . and . . . Mahcky Pats on ahbdy's wahs. Those ud be the great social benefits for the nation.'

I nodded emphatic approval, but I was troubled by that 'ahbdy'd'. They might get the gist of it as far west as Invergowrie and as far north as Powrie Brae, eastwards no further than Monifeith, and it certainly wouldn't translate south of the Tay ('But then, whu does, Jimmy, whu does?' as Alfie would tell you). I voiced my fears.

'Language, Alfie, language.'

'Eh?'

'Ahbdy'd. You said "Ahbdy'd"'.

'So?'

'So who is going to understand "Ahbdy'd" out in the provinces when we hit them with a state of Dundee Law?'

'Naebdy'd. Yer right, Jimmy.' He enunciated carefully' 'Ahbdy ud.'

'Better,' I said.

'Language yersel' Jimmy.'

'Sorry, Alfie. Be'er.'

'Look, son. It's a state o emergency wur dealin wi. Wull jist huv tae learn them whu wey we speak. If they winnae learn . . . (he drew an index finger across his throat, a dire gesture of finality) . . . they deh.'

I nodded again.

'Sta'e o emergency!' we said in unison.

We have a wheen of Lah Hull climbing atween us, for like all natives, we hold the place in a kind of sacred esteem. We bring visitors here to impress them, especially if they don't know the lie of Dundee's land. I learned the place on Sunday afternoons, because Sunday afternoon was tea at Auntie Meg's, and Auntie Meg's house was as much in the shadow of the Lah as ours was in the shadow of the Hully. Her door key hung on a string inside the letterbox and her coal bunker was in the kitchen. Dundee from the tap o the Lah on Sunday afternoons made my childhood self glad that Dundee was where I lived. Its grey-brown familiarity was all around, its river unfurled heroically to the sea, its fields swelled into hills and its hills into blue distant mountains.

'It's wur Sinai' Jimmy,' Alfie was saying, 'wur holy grund.'

He held up one Apostolic hand:

'It's wur cathedral, Jimmy,' he exulted as we peched up on to the plateau top, which was mercifully deserted. He started to run, a thing he did both rarely and unconvincingly, then stopped halfway across the summit, spinning wide-armed like Julie Andrews.

'Wur nave!' he bellowed and ran on.

'Wur quehr and wur presbytery!'

He ran up to the war memorial, a mighty monstrosity but as familiar now as the hill itself. He patted it, kissed its cold stone and stood back, one arm raised open-palmed:

'Wur spehr!' he beamed.

He clasped his stomach with both hands, one on top of the other, bowed his head and began to walk round the new stone-built terrace which is part of the touristification of the place, forbye the 'Dundee Law' signs.

'Wur southern ambulatory!'

He strolled, monkishly contemplative, until suddenly he lifted his head and saw the river, widening through blue and bluer miles to the far off sea-haze. He bellowed:

'Wur pièce de résistance, meh Dundee amigo – wur east windie!'

I believe in the wisdom of working with the sun, likewise the folly of working widdershins. I stir my porridge sunwise, or anything else which requires a stir – a swilled whisky, scrambled eggs, Angel Delight. I walk the Orcadian standing stones of the Ring of Brodgar sunwise and you could not pay me to do it any other way for fear of offending that holy company. It is the law of nature, and over the years of working in nature's midst and writing about it, nature has become the religion of my life, and my poorly defined God is the shaper of nature and the author of its laws. We say 'clockwise' when we mean sunwise. The first clocks were nothing more than the movement of shadows round flat discs. If you were a Lah Hull kestrel hovering high and looking down, you could tell the time by the war memorial's shadow as it circumnavigated the summit. So this exploration of the city from the Tap o the Lah is a sunwise exploration, and it begins in the east because the sun begins there.

At dawn, the North Sea horizon is a hard slatey delineation, and the Bell Rock Lighthouse which sits on top of it is brown. All sources of light lie behind and beneath that singular vertical, tiny and stubborn and thirty miles distant. You need the hard-line-horizon dawns to see it.

The hilltop air is cool and unmoving. Dundee is autumnally clad in low slivers of mist. It is also still streetlit and ungalvanised. It galvanises later on a Saturday. Mostly we don't have time for dawns. We watch more sunsets than sunrises. But we watch more sunrises in Dundee than most places, because Dundee is so good at sunrises.

The trouble with sunrises is their speed. There is the first sinister reddening of the lowest sky, and that seeps into the furthest sea. Then (if it's a good sunrise) the thing explodes, the sun balloons above the lighthouse, the sky rages, the sea mimics, then suddenly it's all pale yellow and too bright to look at and you want to spool it back and start again. There is no afterglow which can consume a lingering western hour at sunset, just business-as-usual daylight. But it has been good to be at the Tap o the Lah from that moment when the brightest light was the flicker of the Bell Rock until the sun bullied its way up past that puny man-flicker; and sometime in the midst of the sun's showy entrance the lighthouse was switched off and you never saw it stop.

Other lights have been aglow in the night, for that low-slung shore between Dundee and Arbroath is a mariner's landscape, familiar to a thousand years of ships from Viking invaders to tomato-soup oil-rig supply vessels, by way of clippers, cutters, barques, whalers, sealers and every species of steamer imaginable. The Vikings, under a general called Camus, put ashore long enough to try and conquer Scotland, although from this distance Barry seems an unlikely battlefield for such an objective, a mile inland from the dark low thrust of Buddon Ness. I remembered a hilariously po-faced Victorian account of the battle in a battered old book called *The History of Dundee from the Earliest to the Present Time* which used to inhabit my parents' bookcase beside *Reader's Digest Condensed Books*, a huge American edition of an English dictionary, a set of *Children's Encyclopedia*, a couple of Daphne du Mauriers, and a mysterious teach yourself book on psychology. Last year, I came across a signed first edition of the same history book, the first I'd seen for perhaps thirty-five years, found that it was dated 1847, and I reacquainted myself with James Thomson's reading of the Battle of Barry of 1010:

> Effectually to rouse the Danish soldiers, it is said, that on disembarking, Camus destroyed or sent away his ships, thus showing his army that they were to rely wholly upon their swords. The morning of the day of battle at length dawned, and the Danes confidently expected to gain the victory; but instead of Scotland becoming a feudatory or dependent of the Danish crown, victory sat on the helmet of her monarch, and hurled defeat and over-whelming disgrace upon the arms of the north . . .

There is yards of this stuff, followed by the bleakly dismissive historian's cop-out: 'Nothing further of importance occurred in which Dundee had any share until the year 1057 . . . '

But Mr Thomson's book has its moments, and because it was the only Dundee history book of which my childhood self was aware, and because it sat permanently askew on a stoorie shelf of my subconscious all these years, it will resurface in these pages. Chapter headings include such appetisers as 'Particular Account of The Church of the Blessed Virgin as it was before the Conflagration'. You have been warned. It is immortality of a kind, I suppose, to have your book invoked 150 years after publication on a dawn hilltop just as the headland of Buddon Ness hardens out of the darkness.

The nearer headland, with its tower house castle where Buddon Ness has a lighthouse, is Broughty Ferry. The haze which slips in from the sea as the sun climbs blurs Buddon Ness out of the view and throws the Ferry into sharper-focus, emphasising its peninsular nature. From this distance, it is not hard to imagine the Ferry's old self-containment; a bowsprit to Dundee's seagoing hull, joined by the community of the river, but remaining its own place. There would always be days – there always will be days – when the haar or the snow curtains off the rest of the world from the Ferry and sets it adrift on the firth with its castle for a fender. To be at home inside

30

the place then is to know briefly and incompletely the self-contained contentment of the islander.

The sun climbs and crawls towards the south, and my mind slips its moorings back to the August heatwave day with Alfie, and the way he seized on one of Dundee's more incongruous set piece landmarks. Back in the days when you could slip out of the East Station to Broughty Ferry by train or venture improbable eastward distances to the seductions of Carnoustie by bike, facing no greater risk than catching your front wheel in a tram line, you had to creep fearfully past the squatting stubby giant of the gasholder and its troubling smell. It was always the price you had to pay if you were a west-ender crossing Dundee en route for the ozone. I have always regarded it ever since with an offended eye, until one blazing day when Alfie spied down from the Lah Hull with his binoculars and alighted on its rusting ugliness.

'Eh speh,' he began without lowering the glasses, 'wi meh little eh, somethin beginnin wi S.F.P.J.' I knew Alfie's S.F.P.J. of old, knew that it stood for his one yardstick of artistic approval – 'sheer fuckin poetry, Jimmy'.

'Where?' I demanded, already fearing the worst, for the wretched thing was all the focal point there was down the sightline of his glasses. He pointed, confirming the worst.

'Burnt umber,' he said. 'Mark Rothko, 1953.' I looked through my own glasses. The rusting flanks of the most grotesque cylinder in town shaded from almost black at the bottom to almost orange where the rust had begun to seep up the white-painted top tier. He squinted sideways at me from the eyepieces.

'Sceptical. Eh can tell a sceptic when Eh see ane. Jesus, fur a published poet yer poetry's affy thin on the grund.'

There's more to Alfie's seeing eye than meets the eye. A bit of him stumbled out of the last of the shipyards into the enlightenment and liberation of a late start in art college, where he had his life coloured and his horizon-wide-open eyes lit by the horizontal swathes of the Russian-American Mark Rothko. Once he presented me with a prized catalogue of a memorial exhibition in Venice in 1970, the year of Rothko's death.

'Look it up, Jimmy. You'll find the gas tank.' When I told him how long I had trembled in the ugliness and stench of the thing,

31

he said. 'Beauty, Jimmy; is in the eye of the gasholder.'

So I looked it up and I found what he meant. It was called 'Purple, White and Red', 1953, and the purple held a good deal of dark-brown rust, and the red held a strong tang of orange rust, and even though the dark shades were at the top, the white in the middle and the orange at the bottom, it was the simplest of mental gymnastics to reorder their horizontals into a mildly abstracted gasholder as seen one summer's day from the Tap o the Lah.

In the hey day of his artistic life, when Sidney Goodsir-Smith voiced the pearl of all his reviews pronouncing in *The Scotsman* that he was 'the poet of the bunch' among his contemporaries, Alfie would ruffle the art establishment's feathers ('easy done, Jimmy, easy done') by growling at private views of this sculptor or that painter: 'Art? What the fuck does he ken aboot art? Eh've built ships!'

Once he stopped me dead when we walked out ablow the Seedlies and offered a five-minute impromptu lecture about the texture and chiaroscuro of a field of neeps. He has opened my eyes, too, in his way, but I never learned to open mine the way he opened his. He'd built ships, you see.

So that bit of Alfie which is my eye-widener, my seeker of poetry among gasholders, sent me questing among the waist-high summer grasses near the hilltop to put a long-lens on the Rothko-esque brute so that I might photograph it in its cityscape context. And being more attuned to the nature of things than the human nature of things, I found myself diverted by the tall grasses, which is part of the same wildering-of-the-Lah-Hull policy as the tree planting. It's not, incidentally, that I object to the tree planting, and I like the strewn birches fine, but I don't think stitching little parcels of dense pine on the hillside has much to do with planting. But this encouragement of the natural grasses and flowers is a fine enhancement. By late August, the grass has grown gold and crackling through the heatwave, with clinging goldfinches and sparrows, and I sat in their eye-level company and was mesmerised. I parted a vee among them and poked the lens through at the sea, and lowered its scope until I had painted the Rothko on to the landscape, and the gasholder in the camera viewfinder was not the monster I cowered before, and it has never been since. Did I ever thank you for that, Alfie?

The sun has reached the south, standing high and sweating, and the city gasps and throws the heat back up at the sun. We are well accustomed to sunlight in Dundee, for it's among the sunniest of Scottish shores where we bide, but not the heat. It is a well-tempered fireball which scribbles round our skies, not this misplaced Californian orb stuck in its month-long hothouse rut. Its heat pulls in the horizon from every direction, a haze on a drawstring, and pales Dundee's portion of the Tay to blue-white creased silk where midstream yachts flounder for want of so much as a sniff of a breeze. Hereabouts it's not natural.

The road bridge looks vertical from here, a corrupted horizontal and 'parallel' to the cathedral spire of St Paul's which has mysteriously aligned its distinguished Gothic revivalist self with that 1960s concrete disaster. Dundee Law has decreed that the bridge should cock itself vertically, and the silly obelisk at its south end recast as its lightning conductor. If only . . . think how much easier it would be to demolish if it were a single tower. Even now, its vertical state has got the scale as wrong as its horizontal reality, not to mention its gate-crashing of the city centre's unique waterfront ambience. It has inflicted blandness on the matchlessness of its setting, and blandness is unforgivable in a bridge.

This kind of reordering of the city's landmarks from above is an eternal fascination as you sunwise circumnavigate the Tap o the Lah. Nearer landmarks glide past further off landmarks as you walk so that you can rearrange them to your liking, through the binoculars or through the composing eye of a telephoto lens. And not all the landmarks are old ones, for Dundee is forever making architectural decisions which it regrets almost at once and spends the next ten or hundred years trying to devise ways of demolishing the result. But in all that fly-by-night company, the square tower of the medieval Old Steeple is the ultimate lesson in building instinctively well and beautifully. I can put my hand on my heart and say that there is much in what is left of Dundee's oldest stonemasonry that I love, but as I have swithered back and forward between Dundee and the rest of the world these last twenty-five years, there is a species of contentment in the shadow of that robust old throwback which I have encountered nowhere else. It has survived the sacking of the city by Cromwell's crowd, sundry lesser squabbles, the fire of 1841 which accounted for its acolyte church buildings, refacing and a degree of rebuilding in the 1870s, and all manner of hideous demolitions and rebuildings in its vicinity since the 1960s.

I don't just love the Old Steeple. I feel sorry for it. I feel compassion for its monumental loneliness, marooned in its permanence among so much transience. I invest it with wisdoms. I hear it silently plead with Dundee's havoc-wreakers:

THE KEY

Whu' wey will ye no
heed o' me? Meh medievalality,
meh ancient stane mentality's
the key

tae free imaginations locked
an rustit. Eh'm the reference point
ye must adhere tae. Appoint
me – eh, me! –

tae be the hopeful antidote
tae mediocrity and worse
– stane poetry in McGonagallised verse! –
and see

can we no rebuild wursels
(beh dingin trashy fashions doon
an thinkin *ahld*) a toon
o heh degree.

I have found a new and unlikely company for the Old Steeple to keep, found it by the Lah Hull's fluke of sightlines, found it because until very recently the possibility did not exist. The selectivity of the big lens has moored the *Discovery* in the same fortuitous frame. At first glance they seem unlikely companions. Yet, are they not both marooned out of their time, astounding survivals of strength and grace and form? We who have inherited them and flourish them as symbols of our city to the outside world should learn from their survival. They are more than PR gestures (although they are excellent PR gestures, too). They are the Burns and the MacDiarmid of the language of our heritage, the evidence of that genius which once flourished in our midst, that genius we should aspire to live up to and emulate. So when I align them both in the same camera viewfinder and try and make sense of what I have joined and why, I feel as sorry for them as I feel proud that they symbolise what my city has been, and what it still can be.

That portion of Dundee crammed between the Lah and Old Steeple is still coloured by the city's industrial lineage. Strange that jute sacks should so closely resemble the muddy shade of stone that built 'the muhlls'. Many a muhll has gone, of course, but scanning the rooftops from the high ground reveals how many survive. Some look deceptively benign in their varying states of decaying indolence or repatriation as homes for the descendants of their slaves. The mighty jute barons would hardly have credited that as a fit or ultimate fate for their immense industrial endeavours, the mice returning after the death of the fat cat to set up home in the cat's basket. You see the long slabs of their walls, the gaunt unbroken slate pitches of their rooftops and, if you are old enough, you remember. I am just old enough to remember a bus stop in Lochee Road where the noise from the jute mill roared and clattered through the stone walls and the bus windows, a grey wall of unearthly sound that made me squirm in my seat and put my teeth on edge. There was a mile of Lochee Road then (to which the no. 17 bus home was enslaved) when you were never out of sight or sound of such walls, such noise and, oh, the blessing of the climb up Tulideph Road into the wholly benevolent force field of the Hully. It was like a reprieve from drowning.

In all this rooftop scanning, one darker, more sinister shape than all the others coalesces out of the mass and seems to stand forward. Its roof is not intact. It is built round a dark courtyard which even this high-noon mid-August sun cannot mitigate or brighten. Of all the adornments with which the jute barons inflicted their egos on their mills, this is surely the most bizarre – a stubby square tower, prototype goon box of a hundred bad Second World War films. The shape of the building, and the death of a mill lass whose hair caught in lethal machinery, conspired against the Logie Works. Its immortality and infamy is in the name the people conferred upon it – the Coffin Mill.

I used to shudder in its shadow whenever duty (never choice!) required me to cycle past it. The muhll buildings have met many a fate, from desirable-ish residences to smoked-glass-windowed supermarkets. This one is a caster of shadows.

The sun, the binoculars, the camera swing past the Coffin Mill, to alight on *the* Tay Bridge, the railway one. What Dundonian of the last hundred and a bit years does not count it among their earliest most abiding and endearing images of the place; the great and graceful familiar, the one good consequence of the Tay Bridge disaster of 1879. Of the three bridges Dundee has thrown across the Tay, this is the only one they got right. The failings of Thomas Bouch's first railway bridge are immortal. McGonagall saw to that, although even without his half-crazy (but only half!) poetry and its baffling survival, it remains the most poignant and visible news story ever to emerge from this journalist-rich city. Even now, almost one hundred and twenty years after the event, the tide lays bare its permanent memorial, the piers which so briefly sustained the fallen girders. Once, when I was very young, their purpose was explained to me, that dark and orderly row in the lee of the bridge. Somehow, the way children do when death is being discussed, I got the wrong end of the stick, and for several childhood years I was convinced they were gravestones, that their dead slumbered somewhere under the Tay's grey waves. Now that I think about it, it's close enough. Seventy-five people drowned in the Tay Bridge Disaster. Fourteen more died in the building of the second bridge. So there is much beneath the Tay which requires that visible memorial of the old piers. But the railway bridge which does survive overcomes even the grief which put it there with its endless and eternally graceful curve, and the affectionate gratitude which all of us who grew and grow up with it greet its reassuring profile.

The road bridge, like so much 1960s concretion, is the wrong profile in the wrong place, gatecrashing our waterfront and, short of building a revolving hotel on the top of the Lah (now what have I said? – someone will think it's a good idea), there is no greater sin which could be inflicted on Dundee's landscape. Alas, it provided the precedent which has permitted countless inflictions where once we walked alongside ships. But more of that anon. For now, from Alfie's Lah Hull, there are two-and-a-bit bridges straddling the silken firth, and I love the one-and-a-bit as much as I despise the other.

More rooftops, a dense grey thicket of them towards the south-west punctuated by trees in green clumps. Emerald and slate work well together, they always have. Dundee is greener than most cities, the Lah reminds you. And it also lets you pick a pocket of rooftops like this perched against the widest swathe of the river, so that if your mind's eye is up to the task and if you know the northmost Scottish outposts of Dundee's whaling heydays, you could be looking down on Stromness from Brinkie's Brae, or Lerwick . . . seagoing places all of them, and you can tell by the rooftops and the cut of their jib.

There is, among all this roof-scanning, a higher, climbing and red-tiled clutch of neatly ordered streets on a flank of the Hully in the west. The highest of all the rooftops is Saggar Street, and the top floor of the highest rooftop was the room with the view of the Bell Rock, where the Crumley family whiled away the 1960s and I discovered the Shadows and turned my back on the piano my mother had ensured I'd studied from the age of seven, picked up a guitar, and resisted the Beatles dynasty by clinging stubbornly to music as defined by Hank Marvin. The Shadows have disbanded, but recently I took my son, Euan, to a Hank Marvin concert. Euan also plays guitar, a guitar which looks remarkably like a Fender Stratocaster, and if you need that allusion explained, you weren't thirteen in 1960 and ripe for the exploitation to which I so willingly succumbed. Ah, you had to be there. Rooftops are a confusing trigger of memorabilia.

Behind that house, still, is a field left wild, kestrel-scoured and corn-gold in this sunlight, climbing to the thick-treed familiarity of the Hully. A snatch of a silly song, performed by an ancient but robust male voice is in my ear . . .

Comin ow-er the Tey Brig tae Bonnie Dundee,
The Braes o Balgay and Lah Hull fine tae see.
Oh meh hert is sae fuhll, there's a tear in meh ee
Comin ow-er the Tey Brig tae Bonnie Dundee.

It belongs, more properly, to the era of stone hot-water bottles and Fry's Five Boys, but it resurfaced in a 1985 cassette of Dundee ballads called *Coorse and Fine*, and it was sung by Stuartie Foy, and he could have been Alfie in meh hoose at New Year God knows how many New Years ago. Stuartie's no Kenneth McKellar, but his rendition is definitive, foot-tapping-on-bare-lino swaying-in-your-seat definitive. On the Tap o the Lah, for reasons I don't care to scrutinise or admit to, I've slipped the tape into a personal stereo in my pocket and Stuartie's voice seems to rise right up out of the grund, so hewn is it out of the stuff of the Lah itsel. Like being thirteen in 1960, you had to be there.

Across the valley where Lochee lies, the Hully smoulders in August bottle-green, the tranquil permanence that was the rock of all my young years. I look at it now with the wide miles of the Tay to the south, the wider miles of Angus to the north, the red roof, the gold field, and while there is no longer a tear in meh ee, there is certainly a lump in meh thrapple. I owe that place; and wherever I wash up, home, as I think of the word, lies somewhere in that thatch of high trees.

Alfie straggled up towards me. Leaving me to my composing, he had gone to scratch at his allotment for an hour or two. All the Lah Hull's sun-facing slopes wear a belt of allotments about the waist. This continuous mile of shanty-town fertility lies like the rock band on the south-west face of Everest, an arresting barrier to be negotiated. You wouldn't credit Alfie with a gardener's skills at first glance, but then allotment work is not gardening. For a start, it doesn't have to look pretty. A mile of allotments is not so much landscaped as purposefully unlandscaped. De-landscaped might be a better description, given that there was a landscape here once and it has been removed so that the allotments might flourish. I like them. I like the tribe of mountain-out-of-molehill miracle workers who tyauve there for a morning, ahld boys stripped off to their Italianate tans who wander up the Lah for a lunchtime hour with their shirts on but unbuttoned, contentedly contemptuous, as they pass the stressed-out reps making frowning phone calls in their parked Mondeos.

Alfie is their archetype. He greeted me with a forefingerful of flicked brow-sweat:

'So how's yer ruminations progressin wi'oo' the inspehrin impetus o meh intellect tae sustain them?'

I told him about Stuartie Foy and the lump in the throat. He shook his head sadly.

'Yer sick, Jimmy.'

38

'Aye, you can mock, Alfie. But I mind New Year, God knows how many New Year's ago, and you singing the self-same song, and your eyes closed so we couldnae see how red they were.'

Then, Alfie was smiling again and clapping my shoulder as if I was his bairn.

'Uv coorse yer right, Jimmy. Yer absolutely bloody right.' And away we went over the plateau bellowing at the top of our voices and in no agreed key in particular,

'Comin ow-ur the Tey Brig tae Bonnie Dundee
The Braes o Balgay an Lah Hull fine tae see . . .'

'No fine tae see, Jimmy, grand tae see . . . from the top.'

'The Braes o Balgay an Lah Hull grand tae see . . .'

'Aye, no bad, but yer needin tae soften that d on the end o grand. Jist hint a' i'. Dinnae ge' too elicuti', ken?'

' . . . an Lah Hull gran tae see.'

'S.F.P.J., S.F.P.'

Tourist voices, distinctly transatlantic – a thing you never used to encounter on the Tap o the Lah. So the rest of the world has discovered us, and seems impressed with the up here of it at least, impressed and a touch confused. A Dundee-voiced guide was pointing out landmarks and fielding questions (why are your skyscrapers so low?) with some expertise. We tuned in.

'And what's that garden?'

'Garden?'

'There. You can see the lawns.'

The guide frowned. Alfie and I frowned. We looked down the line of the animated pointing arm, and the only lawn we could see was not a lawn at all.

'Oh, that,' said the guide, smiling and coming to the same conclusion.

'That's the Vehlet.'

'Vellet? What's that?'

'Naw, naw, Vi – oh – let.'

'Naw, naw yourself, Dougie. What I'm looking at is green, not violet.'

And with that, Dougie, was corpsed on the ground, and Alfie and I were hugging ourselves and smothering hysteria, while trying to put ourselves at a discreet distance even though we were barely able to stand. Well, how was the Yank to know that, in Dundee of all places, we'd thole anything so unlikely as a football team called Violet?

Forever thereafter, if Alfie and I ever became embroiled in a misunderstanding, one would say to the other, 'Naw, naw yourself, Dougie, what I'm looking at is green . . .' in our worst American midwest, and if there were others in the company who required to have the whole story explained, we were uncontrollable long before the end.

But now this sun-wise exploration of Dundee under Dundee Law has swung through west into the north-west, pausing in that otherwise undignified quarter to marvel at Dundee's fourth landscape adornment. There is the Lah, the Hully, the Tey Brig, and there is Cox's Lum. It bears no relation to anything else. And now that jute is long dead as the city's mainstay, it is not even attached to anything else. If you tried to get planning permission for such a thing now, the planners would first examine your health records for evidence of insanity. But there it stands, insanely beautiful, and we love its overlordship as we love wur brig an wur twa hulls. Ego made chimney. But the great lum is Lochee's story and must wait its turn. The city reels away northwards, but it is a city of different priorities and possibilities that lies behind the Lah's turned back. Orange pantile roofs creep in, and white harled walls, and spaciousness, and industry, born in the twentieth century rather than the nineteenth, pock marks the place low to the ground and flashy. Its buildings are transient things, its roads forever being realigned. Out of sight of the river, northmost Dundee looks instead to the hills, to the multi-masted superstructure of Craigowl, summit of the Seedlies, and a gentle, yielding barrier through which generations of Dundee trampers have passed in search of the promised land of the Highlands, the Angus Glens and (impossible distances northwards) the ultimate horizon of the Cairngorms.

There is but the north-east left in this circumnavigation of the volcano, and even if your eye was blinded to the fact that two football stadia and their floodlight pylons seem to collide and overlap – which means they are too close together for anyone's comfort – you might wonder at the two blocks of muhl'is (Alfie-speak for multistorey flats), one with an orange stripe down it, the other with a dark-blue stripe. I'm not sure who thought it was a good idea to decorate twenty storeys of architectural rubbish in football colours. Both Dundee and Dundee United have played rubbish in their day but rarely, if ever, have they descended to football's equivalent of the muhl'is. Besides, both have glory days for their fans to remember, whereas the muhl'is were hideous when they were built and they have only got worse.

Bad luck stitched both football grounds into the same street, and these days the case for ground sharing or some form of amalgamation is irresistible, except that everyone resists it. We all have a sneaking interest in the fortunes of the other lot across the road, and we all cling with what passion we can muster on a wet December Saturday afternoon in a Siberia-born east wind to one set of colours or the other. Me? Same as Alfie. Dark Blue from birth.

Chapter Four

Gillie

The pitch was the street, the school playground, the back garden (never the front on fear of painful retribution), the field. The ball was a sponger, a tenniser, a plastic fake (these varied in size and quality from the fiendish flimsies which wouldn't roll a yard in a straight line – but you could mend a burst with a hot knitting-needle – to Wembley Continentals which took the skin off your bare thigh). Or – luxury of luxuries, fruits of a few heady Christmasses – a tub with a leather lace and a bladder. Woolly balls and balloons were permitted in the lobby.

Football is part of the fabric of Dundee, not in the perverted way that it is part of Glasgow, but rather it is a component of the environment like the mud-coloured stone and slate roofs and tall lums, or something to be imbibed from birth like the smell of the sea.

All football. Tin-can football; kick-the-toes-out-of-your-school-shoes playground football; jackets-for-goalposts football; fifteen-a-side in-the-park football; twenty-one-the-winner football; three-and-in football; anyone but Rangers and Celtic football; *Roy of the Rovers* football; *Charlie Buchan's Soccer Gift Book* football; *Wee Red Book* football; Saturday-nights-with-the-*Sporting-Post*-after-a-bath football; Dundee Reserves on a wet November Tuesday night football; the Gay

Gordon crossing for Gillie to nod the winner . . . perfect football. And a man who gave me half a crown on the no. 13 bus going up Loons Road when I was eight and told me he was Billy Steel. I believed him then. I believe him now.

It became compulsory for me from that moment when, some months after birth, it was possible to stand on one leg, swing the other an inch without falling over, and propel anything round across a square yard of blue lino. Perhaps before that. The midwife who brought my 10lbs several ounces into the world remarked to my father that he had 'a football player there'. Football coloured most of the shades of childhood and youth. Not even the discovery of guitars and girls could swerve my loyalty. But I could hardly have foreseen that football would ultimately proffer my passport out of school into journalism, thence (after an arduous apprenticeship of twenty-four years) into a new existence as a writer of joined-up stuff in books.

My pedigree had a lot to do with that. I forget now how old I was when I learned in childhood that my grandfather had been a pivotal figure in Dundee's footballing history. But to discover that he was the famed goalkeeper of Dundee's only Scottish Cup-winning side – in 1910 – was to be handed a pearl of status among my peers which has served me well ever since. So, inevitably, when I started to play football seriously, I gravitated by way of a magnetic pull to my inheritance between the posts. Alas, I was no Bob Crumley, no Bill Brown either, but in my first game for Harris Academy's first team, I rubbed shoulders with embryonic genius. He was the opposition's centre-forward, and he came with a fearsome reputation. We lost (I think) 10–1. The doubt centres on the one. He scored five or six and had a shot which frankly terrified me, and he unleashed it from the most improbable distances. He made my life and my centre-half's an unthinkable misery. Yet I admired what I saw immensely, even enviously. As the centre-half and I consoled each other after the game, I said:

'So who is the sod, anyway?'

'Him? Peter Lorimer.'

Within a couple of years he was playing for Leeds United (after Dundee had mysteriously turned him down, one of the club's more spectacular blunders) and embarked on a career which would put his name and his goals on the lips of the football world for club and country.

Shortly after that encounter, a few weeks before my seventeenth birthday, I spent two days being interviewed for a job as a journalist with D.C. Thomson, newspaper publishers of legend. The ordeal included a grilling by the editors of (in turn) the *Courier*, the *Evening Telegraph*, the *Weekly News*, the *People's Journal*, and the *Sunday Post*. To a man they asked me the same first question:

'Crumley? Any relation to the goalkeeper?'

Beamed approval greeted my answer. Two weeks later I went to work at the *Courier*.

I never knew my benefactor. He had left home when my father and his five brothers and sisters were very young and their mother was dead. My own mother told me late in her life, and years after my father had died, about a solitary encounter soon after they had married:

'Dad and I were walking in Lochee when he pointed out a man across the street and said: "There's Bob Crumley." '

That was all.

I think of that moment often. I know nothing of the circumstances when Bob Crumley was parted from his family, only that it embittered his children so that they would never speak of him, and that he seemed to have hero-worshippers and detractors in more or less equal numbers. My father seems to have been among the detractors, but I suspect that only because of what Mum told me. Dad did not say 'There's my father'. He did not usher his new wife across the road to meet his father. He said only, 'There's Bob Crumley,' and they walked on.

I was lucky with my football. I first watched Dundee as a child of seven, around 1954, and saw piece by piece the assemblage of the side which, in the early 1960s would announce the club's brief and beautiful golden age. At its best, it would read:

Liney, Hamilton, Cox; Seith, Ure, Wishart; Smith, Penman, Cousin, Gilzean, Robertson.

It was a team of many felicities and distinctions, and, at number ten, one phenomenon . . .

'Gillie,' he said, and in his voice was the kind of reverence you imagine Moses employed, warming himself by his bit bush on Sinai. I nodded. I kenned fine who it was. He kenned better.

'Do you mind the day Gillie came?'

He paused and I nodded again, reluctant participant.

'D'ye mind the . . . the gap?'

The gap? What gap? What was he havering about?

He was searching what passed for a brain, looking for a word. Then he found it and grew articulate.

'The *cred-i-bull-ity* gap . . .'

He was proud of the word, placing the syllables with care, corrupting only one vowel, remembering to pronounce the 't' which is rare hereabouts.

' . . . atween whu we'd kenned afore then whu we seen efter – wi wur ain een.'

He moved a pace closer, frothing his mouth with beer because he drank as he stepped and the co-ordination of it was wanting.

'Maybe you're too young to mind, son?'

So I looked again at the photo on the wall that was just one of hundreds that hung there. It was black and white, of course. All the pictures I ever minded of Gillie were black and white. His was a black-and-white era.

And no, I was not too young. I minded fine. How many years, though? Thirty-five? No – 1962 – thirty-four more like. I'd be, what? Fourteen?

The photo. Had I not cut that very photo from the *Courier* and pasted it into a scrapbook of brown paper pages? Gillie's was a brown-paper-pages era, too. It was the photo of a tall slim man, dark hair high on the forehead, that kind of high on the forehead which would recede too fast. He was in mid-jump. Both arms raised high above his head. Both hands spread wide. Both feet far, far off the ground. That was his gift in the early days, getting higher off the ground than other mortals (meagre creatures like full-backs and centre-halfs), that and the timing of the jumping. The smile – no, the ecstasy – galvanised the dark and placid face (was it not the goal that won the league championship?). The face of a hundred youthful dreams. Gillie.

'There wis ae day he wisnae there then ae day he wis . . .' the voice at my shoulder was saying and, as I turned to meet its face, I saw the barman smile behind its back, shake his head, raise his eyes to the wood-panelled roof and turn away. I knew that sequence of gestures.

46

I had seen in it in a thousand such bars enacted by a thousand such barmen all across the world. Now that I was back in 'meh ahld hame toon' and reunited with this, the first of all my bars, I recognised it again. It said, wordlessly, in all the world's languages which have a word for 'pub':

'You are the victim of a harmless ritual of this place. Ritual is ritual. Intervention is pointless. Your only escape is to be rude and leave. You won't do that because you were brought up to be polite. Besides, you have hardly touched your drink and you were brought up not to waste your food. You're stuck with him and his ritual and the rest of us can't help you.'

So . . . there wis ae day . . .

'Ken the way the haar enveigles itsel up the Tay fae the sea in the night, soondless as snaa?

'Ken hoo ye wake an the dullness o waveslap on shingle stanes is a mark o the difference o the day afore yiv seen it?

'Or – ken hoo the snaa itsel drahs doon the braes like curtains hingin aff the hulls? An the very *quiet* [he sounded the word kweh-e' hunched his shoulders to his ears, slitted his eyes to points of Arctic ice and raised one thumb and forefinger to his face so that thumbtip and fingertip were a quarter of an inch apart . . . all this to emphasise the profound measure of the snow-quiet]

' . . . the very *quiet* wakes you an the room's no as dark as it should be?

'Ye step oot intae the Ferry streets an the pliss is ah whusht an wan an ye wahk among athin that's familiar . . . '

At this he paused as though he had suddenly remembered the glass in his hand, swigged at it with the timidity of one accustomed to making a single pint last a long lunchtime. I raised my own glass but his hand fell on my arm and stopped the rise of the glass. In that hand-on-my-drinking-arm posture he resumed with a dramatically-contrived stage-wheeze:

' . . . but athin's *cheenged*! . . .

'Ye try an reconvene the ahld familiar street in yer heid, just as it was yesterday wi'oo the snaa. An' fur the meenit, ye cannae?

'Well, son, that's what it wis like when Gillie came.'

He led me then by the arm past the pub fire, past hundreds more photo faces, remembered, half-remembered, half-forgotten, hopelessly forgotten, till we stood in front of a second photo of Gillie.

This second Gillie was as high off the ground as the first, but the body was a tall curve like a vertical boomerang. The feet were together and thrust forward, the legs rigid. The curve was at the waist. Back, shoulders, neck and head were supremely aligned in a single purposeful equipoise.

He always seemed to have so much forehead. His imminent balding only partly explained that: the rest was timing. There was no telling from the photo who was being made to suffer. All that was certain was that such a leap, such a header, was bound to have been unstoppable.

'Look. Nijinsky in studs.'

I looked and nodded and laughed, and he approved of the laugh by releasing my drink.

'Onywey, ae day, thir'd been the Dee playin awa week efter week . . . no playin bad, guid fitba . . . we aye played guid fitba in thae days, but jist no guid *enough*.

'What was missin was the . . . the . . . [he cued another word to be relished] *in-can-desc-ence*. Ken what Eh'm on aboot, son? The play was guid, but it wis . . . *cold*. The *spark* wis missin.'

He nodded at the photo.

'That spark. Gillie. Ae day there he wis, an fae then on, the Dee were *in-can-desc-ent*.'

The Dee. Two words to lumpen the thrapple. Dundee F.C. Dark-blue shirts and white shorts, the same strip as Scotland; Dens Park, the tannoy mixing up '*Kon-tiki*' by the Shadows and '*From a Jack to a King*' by Ned Miller with Jimmy Shand playing the '*Bluebell Polka*' and, just as the Dee ran out, '*Bonnie Dundee*'; the guff of fags on an east sea wind that smelled of snow; a Wahlusses peh (we all called them that, no matter how thick or elocuted the tongue in our heids – Wallace's was Wahlusses and pie was peh) steaming in one hand, the strange friendly printer smell of the flimsy blue-and-white programme in the other . . . the commingling scents of Mecca enshrined in the words 'The Dee'.

Hail, hail, the Dee are here
What the hell do we care, what the hell do we care . . .
For it's a grand old team to play for
For it's a grand old team to see . . .

'Goals. Goals like we had never seen afore. Goals that were crafted. He was a goalsmith, son, and he made twenty-four-carat goals. Week efter week, gemme efter gemme, and of coorse it rubbed aff on abdy else. Suddenly, we were winning gemmes, and then we got used wi the feel o winnin. See when you get used wi winnin – ye can beat anybody. We did.

'Won the league. Beat the best in Europe. *Europe*, son! This man put the name of this town – Dundee – on the lips o fitba-playin Europe, and wherever they trehd tae pronounce it – Germany, France, Belgium, Portugal, Italy – ah they plisses – it wis synonymous wi cless. Whu cless we had, son. Whu cless. He did it. Gillie – he wis the spark. Defences owre ah Scotland, owre ah Europe, trehd tae snuff him oot. Couldnae. Ye cannae snuff oot the sheen o gold, ken? They trehd tae hold him doon, kick him doon, knock him doon, pull him doon, and on the rare occasions that beh one cheatin way or other they got him doon, they couldnae keep him doon. Nae mair than they could keep him oot the net.

'Goals. Gillie made goals like Hoagy Carmichael made songs, son. Stardust.

'He made goals like the Picts carved stanes.

'Exquisite!

'Ae year, fifty-three goals. Fifty-three – eessel! Thur's hale teams disnae get that!

'Couldnae keep him of coorse . . . 1964 . . . awa tae Spurs like Buhll Broon afore him. Well, we didnae grudge him that. Ye could-nae grudge Gillie nothin.

'Ken this? It wis a miracle. These een seen it ah . . . plehn's the photie on the wah!

'An ken this – an this is the *real* miracle o it?

'He came fae Coupar Angus.

'Imagine. Coupar Angus, ah berries 'n' coo shit. How'd that happen – wis that the hand o God at work in Hes bloody mysterious ways or whu? That Coupar Angus o ah plisses should calve such a [here was another set-up word to relish . . . I saw the barman silently mouth five exaggerated syllables, 'ah-poth-ee-oh-suss'] such an apotheosis.'

And, right enough, the way he pronounced it he made it sound more a vision of Pompeii than of Coupar Angus. No matter that it was as extravagant a claim to make for a footballer as it was an unwarranted character assassination on Coupar Angus. It was also true, of course – he had come from Coupar Angus, and if the fact seemed a source of wonder, it was nothing more than the norm for the age which produced him.

'It was a time of many strange portents, son. Miracles were in the air. Yuri Gagarin flew in space, mind? America had a Catholic President – ane John F. Kennedy. An the Couparry coughed up Gillie, all in the same year.'

He drew his hand across his brow and flicked away imaginary sweat, symbolic elixir of the adrenalin of 1960. Behind his back, the heard-it-all-before barman mirrored the gesture precisely, mocking him with an unmalicious smile. It was never a malicious howff. How could it be with Gillie on the wall? How can you be malicious in a shrine? Anyway, he came from Coupar Angus . . .

'Ken the Coupar Angus road, son – the Couparry – the Tullybachart Brae sluicin doon tae the berry fields . . . ken the Tullybachart Brae?

'Aye? Bet yiv never drove a horse an cart doon it, eh?'

He had me there.

'Meh granfaither – he wis a drayman, took cartloads o booze doon that brae. Tullybastard he aye crehd it. Niver spillt a drop, though. Whu wis Eh sayin, son?'

The Couparry. Gillie.

'Aye. Well ae day, there wis ae day – '59 or '60, eh? – efter the scout fae the Dee'd been oot tae see the laddie Gillie an says tae eesel, "Wir havin this laddie", – ae day Gillie came doon the Couparry roadie, headed fur Dens.

'Eh want ye to think aboot that journey, son. Think aboot it.

'Now, Eh wisnae there, didnae see him actually traivel. But Eh saw what he did when he got tae Dens. An because Eh saw ah that – never missed one game in fower year, son – Eh've reconstructed his first fateful journey in meh mind a hunner times, refinin it every time.

'Eh hud im doon as Hannibal – Tullybachart wis the Alps – ken that story, son? Elephants plowterin owre they big fancy hulls . . . then he wis a Messiah and there wis fowk wi palm branches ah along the road as far as Birkie . . . Oh, Eh ken what you're thinkin.

Where the hell'd they get palm branches oot at Birkie? — Poe'ic lehscence, son, the fruit o an inspehred imagination.

'Then Eh hud Gillie in the role o Wahlluss . . . no the pehs Wahluss, son, *Wulliam* Wahlluss . . . stravaiglin in owre the fields, layin the land tae waste, goals by guerrilla warfare, leadin by example fae the front, convincin comrades they could win again. That's the image Eh liked best of Gillie.'

A small parliament of regulars had drifted in during the first hour of the pub's morning opening so that now, by noon, they had thickened into a loose knot at the far end of the bar. Now, as one man, they stood and applauded the speech, each mouth sculpted into knowing smirks. They had applauded this piece of pub theatre many times. Only the player with the walk-on part ever changed. Today, the day I came home to my first and favourite pub, I had walked on.

The dénouement:

'Ken what, son? Two years ago he wahked in. He wis grey-haired — whu's left o it — but still Gillie, still lookin as if he could go ninety meenits an he says to me: "You'll be the boy that's tellin abdy as comes in here ah aboot Gillie." That's me, Eh says. "Well," he says, "it seems that half the fowk you tell write an tell me aboot you tellin them aboot me. An maist o them say yer a bit o a nutter, but you think Eh'm *it*. So, Eh thinks tae masel, Eh've been a bit o a nutter in meh time n ah, whu wi ah they goals Eh've nutted, so Eh'll jist awa an see this nutter for masel, so here Eh'm."

'That's what Gillie said. Eh'm paraphrasin, uv coorse, but that's the gist. So Eh *hud* tae ask him aboot the journey, ken? Hannibal, Messiah, Wahlluss or whu? Ken hoo it wis, son? Ken whu he says tae's? A bus! A Bluebird bloody bus. Eez baits were in a broon poke on eez knees. That's whu Gillie said, right here, son, and that's the God's honest truth.'

'It's bugger all of the kind,' the barman bawled out as his patience finally caved in. 'You ken fine. Gillie wis never here.'

'He wiz! He wiz!'

'Then how come naebdy else ever saw him but you?'

'Cos Eh'm in here mair nor anybody else, uv coorse!'

'Ach, yer jist a blahbag. Leave the lad alone, he's suffered enough. Ken whu'll be next, pal . . . he'll be tellin ye ah aboot hoo eez faither played in goal for the Dee when they won the cup in 1910 . . . '

I interrupted the barman.

'Oh, Eh ken that ane,' I said. The barman frowned. The regulars silenced themselves and turned to look. I grinned, put an arm round the shoulders of the storyteller and said:

'His faither. An meh granfaither.'

A pint or two later and more whiskies than I can remember, I asked him:

'So did Gillie really come in here, and did he really tell you about the journey?'

'Naw. But *they* cannae be sure. They've never tae ken.'

'Fine by me. So you made up the last bit?'

'Not exactly. Mind your cousin Annie fae Kettins? She telt me. She wiz on the same bus.'

Chapter Five

The Beau'iful Gemme

The 1990s are not the 1960s, when the Dark Blues bestrode Europe and regularly stuffed Rangers and Celtic (both of which are as much dispehsed – the 'peh' word again – hereabouts as they dispehs each other thereabouts. One thing we cannot tolerate in Dundee is intolerance). Adherence to the cause is more tribulation than triumph. The adherents are conspicuously fewer. It is hard to work up a lather of anticipation at the visit of Ayr or Airdrie if you remember the visit of Cologne or Anderlecht. Yet for me there is one untarnishable joy to assuage, the more or less permanent state of mourning which afflicts all those of us who 'mind o Gillie'. It is that when I slip on to a familiar bench at the Provost Road end at Dens Park – the Provie – I can taste where I come from. That same Dundee which gave me the thirst for nature which I would slake among ever more uncompromising wilderness, has also given me this. This hearth-warmth. This anchor.

Here on this dark-blue-and-white-painted bench, halfway down and a little to the left of the goalposts and half an hour before kick-off at the first home game of a new season, I can sense my father's presence at my side twenty years after he died. There is a companionable essence in the air, as tangible as salt air at the Ferry. With the stockade of Dens Park around me I am beyond the blast and eddies of life's other winds. Here is a still centre where for two hours at a time my head fills with images of family and friends and footballers and the Dundee I grew up with. 'Goin to the gemme' involved them all. The fact that I now go mostly on my own only intensifies the association.

My father is the principal player in these scenes, the figure through whom all footballing associations passed. It may sound an extravagant claim to make for a football ground, but now that so many of the buildings which landmarked the Dundee of my child-hood have gone, Dens Park is the one scalp-tingling, throat-tightening continuity I can still pay homage to. It has been more than forty years. It is not, then, the football fanaticism of the baying, gesticulating hordes that I cling to here, but football as family tradition, the best part of a hundred years of it. Norrie Price, author of Dundee Football Club's centenary book *Up wi the Bonnets* notes that when Scottish international goalkeeper Billy Muir moved to Bradford City in 1907 'Lochee lad Bob Crumley was to prove a worthy successor'. In the second cup final replay of 1910, with Dundee clinging to a 2–1 lead against Clyde, he writes: 'But with Crumley and Dainty out-standing in defence, there was no further scoring . . .' I read such things with a lump the size of the north stand in my throat.

I watch an oldish couple pass by my perch on the Provie Road bench. I know exactly what they will do. They will stop three rows in front of me; he will place the carrier bag on the bench; he will smooth the travelling rug out along the bench so that it provides seating for three; he will sit in the middle, on top of the extra insulation of the carrier bag; she will sit to his right; a second man will join them in a few minutes and sit on his left, on the vacant piece of travelling rug. I smile as this small pageant is played out. Why does such a scene matter to me?

Such people are the building blocks of the club, of the city. They are its mud-coloured stone. They are, like the club, like the city, unflamboyant but sure of their place in their landscape. They are the football fans who prize their football higher than the ones which make the headlines, and so am I. Every club has them and would sink without trace if it did not.

The fact that Dundee's crowds no longer fill Dens Park, and

sometimes they don't quarter-fill it, has created something of an unspoken class structure among the fans. The greater body of fans congregates (and on good days throngs) in the south enclosure. The toffs go in the stand, uv coorse. And the philosophers like myself go to the Provie Road end. I am, admittedly, a Provie Roader from birth, when the 'south enclosure' was little more than a coal bing with steps cut in one side, and the idea of enclosing it with three walls and a roof was as fanciful as floodlights, in other words, a bit . . . well . . . cissy-ish. But as the faithful have dwindled, and as the south enclosure has become the habitat of the rump of the army that was, we Provie Roaders find ourselves with room to breathe, a spaciousness to our accommodation which lets us put our feet up and fosters our philo-sophical bent. Thus, a perfect stranger can turn round, ashen-faced with despair, and exclaim 'Is that no fuckin terrible?' knowing your placatory nod is the consoling fulfilment his philosophy craves.

So it is the first home game of the new season, late August, the Dens Park pitch an unblemished sward, shining as a South Uist machair, and the Dundee strip happily restored to its traditional dark blue and white after a season or two flirting with purple stripes and worse. A philosopher of a kind enthuses at kick-off:

'Come on Dundee, get into this bunch of shite.'

I'm uncertain about his choice of collective noun, but you don't have to be a grammarian to be a philosopher.

I had watched the warm-up, especially the goalkeeper. Dundee goalkeepers, you will perhaps understand, are that tribe of humanity I envy most on the planet, the destiny I never fulfilled. The first of that élite to enter my consciousness, forbye the granfaither, was Buhll Broon, an improbably lanky but robustly gifted genius. When he went to Tottenham Hotspur, he became Bill Brown, but it was Alfie who introduced me to him as Buhll Broon, and I had my first foot-ball hero. His transfer was a black day in my young life.

I was drawn towards goalies; mysterious, idiosyncratic creatures with an individualist's little rituals, tapping the base of the posts with a boot, prowling the six-yard box with a zoo beast's sense of the unnatural confines of territory, stashing small superstitions in the back of the net, death-or-glorying pathetically or heroically. I once played in goal for the 26th Scouts at Riverside Drive, on a winter's day so cold and wet that I arrived home blue and crying, and lay for an hour on the settee with a hot-water bottle. Goalkeeping is football played on the edge.

Where was I? Watching the goalkeeper warm up. He's French, Michel Pageaud, an allusion to Eric Cantona (who is the other Frenchman and absolutely the only philosopher we Provie Roaders have heard of) is somehow compulsory. His first heroics of the afternoon are greeted with:

'Ooh, aah, French keepah!'

But here is a curiosity among the philosophers which hints at an element of Euro-scepticism in our midst. There is no qualm about chanting out first-name plaudits to Dusan (Vrto) or Morten (Weighorst), our other overseas players, but Michel Pageaud remains 'Michael' to the fans. Michel is a girl's name, regardless of how you spell it. The Auld Alliance has its limits, and coyness in the face of calling a goalie Michel is one of them.

Michel's warm-up routine is appropriately different from the rest of the squad, fielding crosses and shots, and ending in what looks to my untutored eyes as a few yoga based contortions. Buhll-Broon, as I recall him forty years after the event, warmed up by blowing on his hands and rubbing the palms together as he ran out. But Michael (as Alfie still stubbornly insists on it) is a class act.

The fan with the bunch-of-shite mentality proves to be the assize the rest of us within his considerable earshot must thole. We have heard him before, of course, and we could either tell him to shut up or move, but we do neither. We sit still and we thole him, him and his uninterruptable fountain of shite two rows behind my left ear. It is not just shite, it is loud and negative shite. He has negative opinions about every Dundee player's every other kick, absolutely every decision by referee and both linesmen, including hand ball and offside decisions at the far end of the ground, perhaps one hundred and fifty yards away. His one redeeming feature is that his opinions of the opposition are worse. The man is loyal, whatever.

'Keep the bah on the grund, Dundee.

'Aw that's shite. Oo' on yur weeng McCann. Naw – yur weeng . . .

And so it goes on, for the entire match, a majestically sustained diatribe, part commentary, part gratuitous advice, all of it liberally laced with swearing as thoughtless as punctuation marks. He doesn't use commas, he uses shite. Such football bores *always* have placid soft-voiced companions with an overdeveloped sense of sportsman-ship and nicely knotted ties with sweaters on top. They spend the game shushing and trying to stem the flow of shite by reasoning with the man. He gets paler as the shite-peddler gets purpler. Alfie's phrase about 'farting in the face of thunder' springs effortlessly to mind.

Yet there is a warmth here. I wouldn't tolerate him in any other proximity on earth. My stoicism is his companionable comforter. His ritualised abuse, the travel-ruggers' ritual, my habitual half-hour pre-match reverie among the littered spoor of my own life and times and my father's which this view of this ground so assists. Is it all not the same thing as the goalie's ritual? The prowling defence of our own territory? Dundee Football Club as the talisman of our own life's endeavours? You see, I told you we Provie Roaders were philoso-phers.

We score direct from a corner in five minutes. We miss enough chances to win five games. The bunch of shite equalises in the last minute: 1–1.

'Yur always the bloody same, Dundee. Week efter week. Year efter year. Yu'll never ge any be'er, Dundee. Never. Never. Yur shite, Dundee.'

He's wrong again. He's been wrong almost every time he opened his mouth for fifty years. He said the same in 1962. We philosophers know, you see, that sooner or later there will be a new golden age. It's only a matter of time. One Saturday afternoon it will dawn. It would not do to be absent and miss it. Deep down, he knows it too. It's why he's here, but he doesn't bother to look deep down to find out. That's the beauty of the beau'iful gemme. Meantime, I watch Michel with quiet admiration and no little envy. I look for portents among every new face to wear the number ten shirt. Is this, could this be, a new Gillie about to flower? The burden of expectation. It's the same in Brazil. For Gillie read Pele.

I am supremely and quite unjustifiably optimistic about Dundee F.C. I forgive them everything in the lean years for all that they have given me in all my years. And I know that every time I see the dark blue and white run out on to the pitch, however the game pans out, sometime in the next ninety minutes there will be some passages of play to admire. We have always produced teams which are capable of playing the game the way God made it. They may not always remember that they are capable of such things, but now and again the current side rise above the mundanities of the modern game and thread together a few moves which acknowledge the tradition both they and I inhabit.

The bunch-of-shite man won't acknowledge it. He'll find fault with it.

'Come on, Duffy, bring on yer substitute,' his accomplice pleads to the manager.

'Substitute?' he bellows. 'He'd be better bringin on a prostitute.'

But when he goes out into the street again, you will say a word against Dundee F.C. or besmirch the Dark Blue at your peril. He shuffles morosely for the exits. The PA cheerfully announces the 3–0 defeat of Dundee United by Dunfermline.

'Ho-ho!' he exults. 'The Arabs got stuffed. No such a bad day then, eh?'

Charity begins at home, but at the Provie Road end, Dundee United is the opposite of home, which means away. The Provie Road is the furthest you can get (about four hundred yards) from Tannadice and still be in Dens Park. So now you know why it makes philosophers of those of us who linger there.

The Bunch-of-shite (see how his vocabulary quickly became his name tag for weekly use by the rest of us within his earshot) was singing much the same tune in November, by which time Dundee were second in the league and, by virtue of an exhilarating sequence of bravura victories, were in the final of the Coca-Cola Cup against Aberdeen. It is the perpetual pursuit of an argumentative strain of misery which keeps him going.

The weekend before the final, we played Dundee United at Tannadice, hell-bent on good omens. It is a fixture to be relished with missionary zeal whatever the circumstances. To go there is to preach the gospel of the cultured game circa 1962 to the infidels who never really learned the trick of it, or so it has always seemed to the Provie Road philosophers. But wait – what's this?

En route to Tannadice I passed the Provie Road turnstiles to find the words AWAY SUPPORT ONLY newly painted above the doors.

What?

Forty-one years, boy, youth and man, cast aside like an empty Bovril cup or a bad pie. What should I do about it? Lodge a written protest? Join the Foreign Legion? Become a United supporter (much the same thing)? I mulled over the dilemma morosely as I took my seat at Tannadice. Life's watersheds, I philosophised, don't insinuate themselves into your psyche, they kick you in the solar plexus when your back's turned.

No Provie Road.

What, never?

Provie Road no more?

The match kicked off, a sell-out nearly.

The crowd uproarious, myself a troubled island of mysterious silence in my new Dundee Football Club tartan scarf, immobile, unanimated.

I looked round. Was I the only one to mourn its passing?

The last instinctive Provie Roader left alive?

Involuntarily, I began re-running films of games past in my head.

Dundee 2, Hibs 2. The first game ever, seven years old and goggle-eyed at the size of the place and the crowd, the first match I'd seen away from Lochee Park. I scratched my head for the names . . . Buhll Broon, Shug Reid mebbe, Doug Cowie definitely, Jim Chalmers on the weeng, Buhlly Burse, Danny Malloy, Hibs' famous five . . . what an introduction to the Provie Roadie. The heroics of the early sixties, winning the league. Cologne! say the word Cologne in Dundee and it only means one thing. 8–1. Europe held its breath that night. Dundee? Who or what or where was Dundee? What power was this unleashed on the football landscape of Europe? Power which could humble the mighty Goliaths of Cologne. Saw it fae the Provie Road.

We beat the Queen of the South in the fog. Thought the score was 7–1. Got home to discover it was 10–3. Gillie'd hit seven. Saw (some of) it fae the Provie Road.

Thirty intervening years of highs and lows, hopes and fears. Some people think football's a matter of life and death. It's not: it's much more important than that. Bill Shankly said that. If his tongue was in his cheek (it wiz, it wiz!) it didn't show. Well, there have been moments during the ninety-plus years that my family has been infatuated with Dens Park . . . this was one of them. Life and death, no.

But under your skin and laying a fair claim to your heart from time to time, oh yes.

The film in my head was running black and white now, a jerky newsreel from 1910. They say when my grandfather came home with the cup (and the rest of the team, mind!) men were handing round their bottles of whisky in the street like it was Hogmanay, only better. Mind you, whisky was half a crown a bottle. Oh, imagine if we bring the Coca-Cola Cup back on Sunday. Whisky in the streets. I don't even know if there was a Provie Roadie in 1910 . . . GOAL!!!

November 1995, Tannadice. I'm on my feet with my hands in the air. How did I get here? The subconscious took over, propelling me upright. The ball is in the United net and we're celebrating.

Ninety-two years. Mebbe more?

Provie Road no more?

Where'll I sit . . . GOAL!!!

I'm up again! 2–0.

'One team in Dundee,

There's only one team in Dundee . . .'

Half-time. I'm singing. Surrounded by several thousand total strangers and singing with them as if I've known them, the nearest ones anyway, all my life. Is that it? Have I to join the crowd, give up being a philosopher and become a singer? What . . . GOAL!!!

3–0. Can it be? It can. It is.

'Come on Dundee,' bawls the nearest total stranger, inaudible in the bedlam to the whole world other than me . . . 'let's give them a real fuckin tankin!' He must be seventy. He's beautifully turned out, dressed by Burberry at a guess, but he's on his feet and he's punching the air and swearing heartily. He'll go home and be a church elder and doting grandfather. What films does he play in his mind?

We didn't tank them. They fought back, scored twice, but only twice, and we held out. 3–2. For an hour there, we were enlightenment, we were missionaries preaching the gospel of '62. Saw it all fae the Provie Road.

Provie Road no more? At least I won't have to sit beside the Bunch-of-shite ever again.

Hampden, sold out, 35,000 fans and half of them ours. Where do they go the rest of the year? How we sang. We lost, 2–0, overawed and outclassed. We had nothing to sing about on the face of it, but we were at Hampden, and we sang. The team came back out with their losers medals and through their tears and our lusty cadenzas, they applauded us.

'We love you, Dundee, we do
We love you, Dundee, we do
We love you, Dundee, we doooooo
Oh, Dundee, we love you.'

Later, in a quiet bar by the Clyde, I shared a consolatory pint with Euan, my eighteen-year-old-son. He's a Hearts man at heart but he'd donned the ancestral colours for the day and sang louder than anyone. Once or twice, too, as the ground filled up I imagined my father sitting next to us. I call his ghost up often, but especially at sporting occasions where I think he would have enjoyed himself hugely. I call up my mother's ghost, too, but for subtler occasions than this.

Euan was disappointed of course. But he'd seen Hampden aflame and we'd sung along to 'Flower of Scotland' with Big Country and a pipe band. Twice near the end, we'd almost scored. You don't forget such hours, ever. And although he was not born in Dundee and has never lived there, he has the gist of the place and the pull of the dark blue from his faither.

But I was numb, still, too quiet for my own comfort. It was only a football match. But I'd lost a cup and the Provie Road in one week and the streets of Dundee would not ring to the carousing of men passing bottles of half-crown whisky round like it was Hogmanay. Not tonight. It's too important for that.

Two weeks later back at Dens, and the Provie Road end is miraculously restored to us. What was that all about? Who cares, I'm back where I belong. The whistle blows for the kick-off, and a voice sounds off in my ear:

'Come on, Dundee. Get stuck into this bunch of shite.'

Chapter Six

His Name was Bill

Lochee's relationship to Dundee is like Scotland's to Britain – hell-bent on stubborn independence but disinclined to disassociate itself completely. Collections of Old Dundee photographs tend to ignore it studiously, or perhaps it was just that Lochee is not the kind of place where postcard photographers find favour. It is an old village turned suburb, a worker's place perpetually accustomed to the dirt under its fingernails.

It used to have its own railway station. The building is still there, a howff for the local Burns Club, an enlightened survival, and all that remains of an outpost of the Dundee–Newtyle railway. It also used to house a tram depot (a thing of evil wonderment, a huge reverberating cavern into which I thrust my head fearfully for I never felt anything for trams but a profound loathing; they could make me sick in ten minutes of clattering travel).

Lochee was never less than its own tenacious place, clinging to the banks of a stone river, the winding mile of its main street. It flattered itself (it still does) by calling the upper reaches the High Street. Dundee makes disclaiming derogatory jokes about Lochee. (What do you call an Alsatian with a collar on in Lochee? A tourist.) Most of them have a pot-calls-kettle-black kind of cheek about them. The truth is that Lochee and Dundee folk are chips off the same block of mud-coloured stone, always have been. Lochee is simply Dundee in microcosm.

Both my parents grew up there. My father and his father were born there, and my mother arrived as a very young child having been born in Rochdale but with two older brothers born in Aberdeen, such was the peripatetic nature of her father's cinema manager career. What the natives made of her elocuted voice is anyone's guess. Jokes probably. But the war's one benevolent act was to provide a prefab for the pair of them up by in Glamis Road on the slopes of the Hully with the view of the river and the welcoming breath of the west wind. Lochee doesn't do views of the river and it's never been particularly strong on fresh air, although that at least has changed for the better since Cox's Lum and its cohorts stopped reekin.

So it was that James Anderson Crumley, son of the goalie, and Nellie Illingworth, daughter of the local cinema manager, decanted from Gray's Lane, Lochee, and climbed the hill out of that small and introverting world. And for all that they never lost their feeling for the place, they were not sorry to be up and out of it either.

But the thread was not cut. That old face peering round the first-floor curtain of a drab tenement at 67 Logie Street (the house now long demolished and a good thing too) cracked into its accustomed grin at the first sight of me rushing downhill from the Anky (the school, not the pub – I was only seven). I think of that face now, almost forty years since I last saw it, and I think of it still with as much affection as I ever thought of any face. He was what Mum had left behind in Lochee, and such was his impact on my young life that no one else's photograph so readily reconvenes my earliest memories. I travel between Dundee and Lochee effortlessly, and without noticing the join, and I think that is as it should be. It is the legacy of the face at the window. His name was Bill, and he was the grandfather I knew.

He lived in a two-roomed tenement with a scullery the size of a decent cupboard (the scullery sink was the only one in the house), an alcove for a bedroom, and a torture chamber for an outside toilet. I loathed that stinking little hell-hole as much as I loved him. I suffered all kinds of squirming indignities rather than

Hat parade – Grampa and Grandma Illingworth (far right) in their courting days

Mum (third from right) in a chorus line, around 1930

Great-Grandma Barrie

Fairy Grandmother – Hauldean Illingworth casts her spell

Mum's first set of wheels, with her brothers,
Stuart and Eric

Merry widow – a favourite picture of Mum

Dad (left) the Desert Rat . . .

. . . and (left) with an Army buddy in North Africa

Dad with truck: Berlin at the end

Lance-Bombardier James Anderson Crumley, Royal Horse Artillery

Me, aged 18, and 'the worst guitar Hofner ever made'

Dad, still smiling, despite the demob suit

Bob Crumley, Dundee FC goalkeeper

Family portrait around 1965: (from left) me, Dad, Mum, and my brother, Vic

'Auntie Meg'

Prefab days: me (left), Vic, and pedal car

Me with cap, decrepit trike and uncertain friend

dare its fearful maw. But there were emergencies . . .

The key hung by the main door of the flat. I unhooked it with all the timidity of a jailer compelled by incomprehensible forces to lock himself in his own cell. It was stone-floored, splinter-seated, cold beyond words, equipped only with newsprint not for reading. It was halfway down the outside stair and it was shared by four households. I shudder now to think how long he must have used it. Forty years perhaps, certainly thirty. His wife, a semi-invalid in her later life, would suffer it for only six years fewer than he did. They both used chamber pots at night.

Once, after his wife died, he came to stay with us for a few days. He kept me awake at night for hours because he talked to himself in bed and I could hear him chew over his problems through the wall. From him I learned a little of what it is to be old while I was still very young.

His name was Bill, Bill Illingworth, which is a conspicuous name in Lochee. I called him Grampa. He concealed from his countless friends in Lochee and as much of the rest of the world as he could the middle name he loathed – Timothy. Surviving in Lochee in his day with a north of England accent (he never lost it, not in the fifty years he lived here) was assize enough to thole without a name like Timothy to gnaw away at your self-respect.

He smoked bogey roll in a pipe he knocked out on the hearth. My brother and I fetched it by the ounce from the paper shop and he worked it with one-handed fluency from the black leather pouch in his cardigan pocket. He peeled apples with a penknife and ate the pieces from the blade. He drank tarry tea without milk, a habit I borrowed and persevered with for ten years simply because he had done it. He made mousetraps out of a square foot of plywood smeared in glue with a piece of cheese in the middle. It was wretchedly efficient. The mouse went for the cheese and stuck. If it wasn't dead in the morning he finished it off without explaining how. He had great admiration for one mouse which regularly and mysteriously reached the cheese. He made sublime rice puddings with a gold and crunchy skin. He held court from a battered armchair before his fire. My brother and I sat in thrall on fender box stools which contained rags and Brasso. The fender shone. He wound the mantelpiece clock daily at 6 p.m. and checked his waistcoat pocket watch against it, a ritual of some gravity. He was a cinema manager but his real business was magic.

Almost every afternoon after school we went to Grampa's and met our mother there and had tea. After tea he told stories out of his head, stories about two cats called Tommy and Tibbie, jungle adventures about Tarzan and Sabu. Jungles fascinated him. The Amazon enthralled him. And because it enthralled him he saw to it that it enthralled us. He had that gift, that way with him. The detail of the stories is gone, except that sooner or later they would feature some spectacular trick whereby Tarzan would confound the forces of evil with the words: 'I am the God of Fire!'

He made us things. There were at least two garages for our Dinkies. There was a switchback track where our Dinkies cavorted. There was a pair of stilts, silver-painted swords, brighter painted shields . . . He whistled Rossini overtures, a wondrous feat, the walls of his cheeks a-tremble at the precision of the execution as he whistled. My first LP was of Rossini overtures.

Lochee was his domain. My mind's eye sees him nowhere else, although old family photographs place him here and there (the brief-case-in-hand businessman *en route* to the bank, the holidaymaker on Carnoustie beach: both pictures show him in soft-brimmed hat and jacket and tie). At various times he managed Lochee's three cinemas – Gray's, the Rialto and the Astoria. Gray's was long gone by the time I was aware of him, but we haunted the Rialto and the Astoria. When bingo usurped them as cinemas, it was as if some vile devilry had been invented to besmirch his memory. It was as well that he did not live to witness the besmirching, for the cinema had been his life from the day he hand-cranked a projector at private showings of the 1905 epic *The Gypsy's Revenge*. Five years later he opened his own cinema, the Hippodrome, in the Hawkhill, and launched a celebrated war with the nearby Magnet. No trick was too low to outsmart the opposition. They vied for children's custom – a free bar of chocolate and an orange at the Hippodrome was countered by a stick of rock and a postcard at the Magnet. It never happened at Mecca Bingo.

He had a coterie. They met not in the pub (as far as I know – I have no memory of him with a drink in his hand) but in Willie McWalter's barber backshop, a Parliament of cronies, solitary men with shopping bans, chinwagging their havers at each other for hours at a time and poking relentless fun at the rest of Lochee beyond their circle whenever it dropped in to have its hair cut.

Their focal point was Willie McWalter himself, and his is the only other face which still springs into sharp focus out of the fag-fug of that place. He was squat and boxer-faced and full of mostly agreeable bullshit. He cut hair with half-moon glasses on his nose and a hand-rolled fag in his mouth. His face, if it wasn't creased with wry mirth at his own unstoppable flow of banter and bad jokes, was creased at the equally unstoppable irritant of the cigarette. He cut our hair to the bone and smothered what was left in a dressing he called 'gutters' which set like a cyclist's helmet. I loved the place, loved its old fogey smells, loved the ritual mysteries and intimacies of its ancient generation.

'Morning, Bill.' Willie McWalter interrupted his own awful story about a bogey man who lived in a cave up the Hully with a knife stuck through his hand – or was it an axe? Like Excalibur it resisted all attempts to pull it out, and presumably King Arthur had better things to do than dally with the Hully's cave dwellers. So there he was. My nine-year-old self was trapped under Willie's barber-sheet having a back-to-school shear on the last Monday of the seeven weekies. I looked up, but the hand not wielding the scissors thrust my half-shaven head down again, just as I caught his grin of recognition in the mirror. Grampa!

'Hullo, Willie. What's that you've got under there? Looks familiar.'

'This ane? Guttersnipe. Ane o they slum bairns fae up the Glammy. Have nothin t'dae wi 'im. E's been petrifehin iz wi some havers aboot an eejit wi a mangled hand, him as bides up the Hully.'

Grampa nodded, and immediately locked into the conspiracy.

'Ah. The Beast of Blackness. The man with two tongues. The police arrested him once but he got off because he pleaded guilty and not guilty at the same time and they couldn't understand either of the words he said. That the one, Jimmer?'

How could they *do* that, I wondered, lost in admiration.

How could one of them walk in cold off the street and plug in at once to the free flow of rubbish, instantly attuned? Willie knew that Grampa was in for a chat rather than a haircut because he didn't remove his hat. I piped up a protest.

'It was Willie. He was the one who wiz petrifehin *me*! It wiz his story aboot the man wi the axe in ees hand.' Willie McWalter jerked my face up into the light by what was left of my hair.

'Look at this, Bill. Does this look like a petrifehd pus to you?'

I giggled again. If I had used a word like pus in my grandfather's company, I would have been grounded for a week without pocket money and my father would have thickened my ears.

Grampa peered down from his hat. 'Nothing but freckles and mischief there. I believe Willie.' And tuppence magicked its way into my clenched palm. It had become a magic room. Willie McWalter and Grampa to myself, sunlight illuminating a roomful of fag smoke and dust and floating bits of hair, coppers in my hand too precious to entrust to my pockets. Willie was havering again.

'So eh wiz up the Hully and the mannie wi the mangled hand comes oot eez cave and says:

"Haw, Wullie. Haw, Wullie," and Eh says, "Whu izzi, Bogey Man?" Eh wiznae feart o the likes o him. If ye dinna let on yur no feart e diznae bather ye. "Haw, Wullie," e says, an e hauds up eez mingin hand and there's the handle o the axe hingin oot, and blood owre ah the pliss.

"Haw, Wullie, you wah'n some o this blood for yer shop, only eh cannae get the blood to stop runnin. Eh've got buckets o the stuff. Maybe you could use it . . . mix it in wi yer gu'ers that ah they wee laddies like, ken?"

"Good ehdea, Bogey Mannie," says eh, an e filled a bucket for iz, an this is Bogey Man gu'ers Eh'm slappin on yer heid.'

And at that he splattered my head with his usual concoction of pale green hair dressing and combed it into my usual concoction of a wave at the front.

'But it's green!' I said.

'E bleeds green,' retorted Willie McWalter and cuffed the back of my head instead of taking the shilling for my haircut. I retreated to the back row of his three-row twelve-seat auditorium and hugged my knees. It was the best day of the whole seeven weekies.

Two more old boys stamped in, a military gait; the gait that stamped their lives forever after the day they learned it, dark bloody day that it must have been for most of them, not that my sunny day's young thoughts knew anything of such gaits, such darkness. Grampa put his pipe smoke on the air and the newcomers mixed it with their Woodbines while Willie moistened another Rizla paper with his tongue and expertly furled one more DIY fag. (He was an infinitely more expert fag roller than a barber. . . . my father's estimate. And when in teenage years, when Grampa was gone and Willie McWalter just as dead or retired, and I went to Dad's barber in downtown Dundee, I agreed with it – but not then, not then!) Today, I couldn't thole five minutes in such a cancerous thundercloud, but then I felt as if I had been elevated into the select ranks of a cabal of heroes. I was vaguely drunk on it all. I watched the smoke ignite in the sunlight and I basked in my grandfather's reflected glory. It occurs to me now as I write that throughout my adult life I have inclined towards the company and friendship of people older than myself, often a lot older. I wonder how much of that inclination is rooted in days like these.

The coalman walked in.

'Wullie!'

'Paddy!'

'Bill!'

'Paddy!'

He nodded affably at the others, acquaintances by sight only. Then he saw me, and his blackened face cracked into its most wondrous smile.

'Whippersnapper!'

'Oh, don't talk to him,' cautioned Willie. 'Eh've hud tae spatter es heid wi blood, he wiz gettin that abstreporous. Usual?'

Paddy was . . . well, Irish, I suppose, although all I knew at the time was that he had a lousier job than anyone else I ever met, and his voice crackled with a kind of music-in-speech that pitched vowels and consonants in very unfamiliar accents. He was huge, with hair like vertical barbed wire. He was our coalie as well as Grampa's. He was perpetually black and his eyes were as deep and soft as peat bogs. But it was his teeth you remembered, or maybe it was just the blackness of the face they greeted you from, bowed beneath his burden as he strode up our path.

'Whippersnapper!' he greeted you, and it was all you ever heard him say to you, though the voice lilted away to your parents, and now it bantered with Willie McWalter in his chair.

Willie now did an amazing thing. He took not scissors and clippers to the coalie's hair, but fire! Somewhere by the sink (my mind can no longer conjure up the source) he had lit a small flame and dipped some kind of taper into it. And with this fiendish thing (and how he could have petrified me up the Hully with fire in his hand! — the incarnation of his own hideous story) he began to burn the coalie's hair away.

I wish now I could peer back down those four decades, peer round the door of that backroom and see the freckled-faced imp in shorts and sandals that was myself; I wish I could watch the horrified fascination on my own face as the flame singed away the coalie's hair, smouldering it down into a manageable thatch. In the fug of the singeing and the thickening cocktail of sun-filtered tobacco smoke, Willie McWalter blurred round the edges; a demon barber with fire in his hand. I retreated further back into my corner and hugged my knees tighter while my eyes widened and Willie's havers of a few minutes before became all too plausible. Maybe it was true about the Bogey Man. Maybe he was the Bogey Man, and maybe it was he who bled green? I looked at my grandfather and wondered if he was part of it, too. If anyone could talk with two tongues at once, he could! I wrestled with the idea. Was it one tongue on top of the other? Or side by side? I tried to imagine what that felt like, and made up two different sentences and tried to hear the sound of both of them at once in my head. But I still couldn't imagine green blood.

There came a lull.

Their blethers faltered.

They stubbed out and lit up again. Grampa fed his furnace using his ancient flint lighter flat across the pipe bowl to stoke the bogey roll into its ripest fragrance.

Willie McWalter was uneasy in the company of silence, but then he still had a wife and would be accustomed to chatter in the evenings by the fire. The others, the solitary men like Grampa, knew silence, that silence they break occasionally by talking to themselves, even in a strange bed.

'S gone affy kwehi,' Willie frowned. 'Bill, gees another chapter o that jungle stuff ye wiz on aboot yesterday.'

Grampa abruptly changed his demeanour. His voice was at once clipped and smooth, his vowels round and southern. He spoke not in his accustomed conversational Lancastrian but in a kind of Victorian travelogue-speak. And as he spoke, in my mind's eye his jacket and hat were no longer workaday grey but safari off-white, sweat stained at the oxters, the small of his back, and at the headband. Without a pause, without a moment's reflection, without any preparation of any kind, Grampa began and talked thus without a break:

'The heat increased rapidly towards two o'clock – 92 or 93 degrees Fahrenheit, by which time every voice of bird or mammal was hushed; only in the trees was heard at intervals the harsh whirr of a cicada. The leaves, which were so moist and fresh in the early morning, now became lax and drooping; the flowers shed their petals. Our neighbours, the Indian and Mulatto inhabitants of the open palm-thatched huts, as we returned home fatigued with our ramble, were either asleep in their hammocks or seated on mats in the shade, too languid even to talk. On most days in June and July a heavy shower would fall some time in the afternoon, producing a most welcome coolness. The approach of the rain-clouds was after a uniform fashion very interesting to observe. First, the cool sea breeze, which commenced to blow about ten o'clock and which had increased in force with the increasing power of the sun, would finally flag and die away. The heat and electric tension of the atmosphere would then become insupportable. Langour and uneasiness would seize on everyone; even the denizens of the forest betraying it by their motions. White clouds would appear in the east and gather into cumuli, with an increasing blackness along their lower portions. The whole eastern horizon would become almost suddenly black, and this would spread upwards, the sun at length becoming obscured. Then the rush of a mighty wind is heard through the forest, swaying the tree-tops. A vivid flash of lightning bursts forth, then a crash of thunder, and down streams the deluging rain. Such storms soon cease, leaving bluish-black motionless clouds in the sky until night. Meantime all nature is refreshed. But heaps of leaves and flower petals are seen under the trees. Towards evening life revives again. The following morning the sun again rises in cloudless sky, and so the cycle is completed – spring, summer and autumn, as it were, in one single tropical day.'

Grampa wiped the small splashes of froth which had gathered about the corners of his mouth as that storm rose and fell. He used the back of his hand, and was dissatisfied with that, removed a hanky from his trouser pocket, dabbed the corners of his mouth, and then, the better to illustrate the tropical setting, removed his hat and wiped his brow, and fingered his collar. I tore my eyes away from him to look at the others. The coalie's eyes were on him in the mirror, Willie was motionless, comb and taper poised in mid-air, wonderingly regarding Grampa over his half-moon glasses, the other two were on the very edge of their seats, one with his chin on his clasped hands, his elbows resting on his knees, the other with hands on knees and leaning forward. This last one now sat back.

'Eh dinna ken how ye dae it, Buhll,' he gasped, 'but dinnae stop.'

Grampa was as fond of an audience as a rice pudding. He began again with a conspiratorial edge which sucked us all in at once.

'We often read, in books of travel, of the silence and gloom of the Brazilian forests. They are realities, and the impression deepens on longer acquaintance. The few sounds of birds are of that pensive or mysterious character which intensifies the feeling of solitude rather than imparts a sense of life and cheerfulness. Sometimes in the midst of the stillness, a sudden yell or scream will startle one; this comes from some defenceless fruit-eating animal, which is pounced upon by a tiger-cat or stealthy boa constrictor. Morning and evening the howling monkeys make a most fearful and harrowing noise, under which it is difficult to keep up one's buoyancy of spirit. The feeling of inhospitable wildness which the forest is calculated to inspire, is increased tenfold under this fearful uproar. Often, even in the still hours of midday, a sudden crash will be heard resounding afar through the wilderness, as some great bough or entire tree falls to the ground. There are, besides, many sounds which it is impossible to account for. I found the natives generally as much at a loss in this respect as myself. Sometimes a sudden sound is heard like the clang of an iron bar against a hard, hollow tree, or a piercing cry rends the air; these are not repeated, and the succeeding silence tends to heighten the unpleasant impression which they make upon the mind . . . '

Grampa eyed each of us in turn. He had us all. It was not Woodbine smoke that sunlight infiltrated but the Amazonian canopy. We were, men and boy, sweating and scared explorers. The jungle closed in.

'With the native it is always the Curupira, the wild man or spirit of the forest, which produces all noises they are unable to explain. For myths are the rude theories which mankind, in the infancy of knowledge, invents to explain natural phenomena. The Curupira is a mysterious being whose attributes are uncertain, for they vary according to locality. Sometimes he is described as a kind of orang-utan, being covered with long, shaggy hair and living in trees. At others, he is said to have cloven feet, and a bright red face. He has a wife and children, and sometimes comes down to the rocas to steal the mandioca.'

We all nodded, some swallowed, as if rocas and mandioca were words we heard every day on the Logie Street pavements.

'At one time I had a Mameluco youth in my service, whose head was full of the legends and superstitions of the country. He always went with me into the forest; in fact, I could not get him to go alone, and whenever he heard any of the strange noises which no one could explain, he trembled with fear. He would crouch down behind me and beg me to turn back, his alarm ceasing only after he had made a charm to protect us from the Curupira. For this purpose he took a young palm leaf, plaited it, and formed it into a ring, which he hung to a branch on our track . . .'

Grampa took out the hanky again, and Willie McWalter laughed and went back to work.

'Tell us again, Bill,' he said, 'what was the nearest you ever got to the Amazon?'

Grampa chuckled.

'Cornwall,' he said.

'Here, you'd better run along, Jimmer,' he told me. 'Your Mammar'll be wondering . . .'

I grinned my gratitude and ran out into the street, into the sunshine, with a shilling and tuppence in my hand, and no boy was ever richer. But on the way home, as I crossed Lochee Park under the Hully, my head was full of the morning's stories, and somehow the Bogey Man and the Curupira had insinuated themselves into the same creature, and I wondered how I might find a palm leaf and whether or not I would be as skilful as the Amazon boy at making a ring out of it, for handiwork was never my strong suit at school. In any case, I was doubtful if it would stop a Bogey Man even if it did dissuade a Curupira from coming down to the rocas to steal the mandioca.

One day I arrived at Grampa's after school as per the ritual to be met at the door by my mother in tears. This was such a staggering event that it struck me not as a sadness but as a great adventure. She would not let me into the house, but gave me the bus fare home, the first coin that came to hand being a florin. Such distraction, such liberating independence was unknown in my life, such a rash dispensation of raw cash barely believable in my mother, who was long accustomed to her generation's magical manipulation of pennies and making them do the job of shillings.

I was sent home, charged with telling my father when he came home from work that Grampa was ill and he should get there fast. The importance of my role was what impressed me at first. I was sitting on the coalbunker by the garden shed when Dad came home. I proudly delivered the message beginning 'Dad! Guess what!' He responded eagerly enough and I saw his face change as my bulletin unfolded, and I saw something then I had not seen before in any face. He left again at once and as I watched his car speed away towards Lochee, I realised I had not told him the other part of my news. I was locked out. But I had not grasped the essential burden of the moment at all . . . that my grandfather was dying.

Grampa's death was the first one to impinge on my young life. He was 80 and I was 10. 'Remember the good times,' Dad advised later that night. But with Grampa there were only good times. When he died the world took away my first hero, and emptied a chair at Willie McWalter's shop. After that, we began to get our hair cut in town.

Years later, twenty of them at least, I found a scruffy book in a scruffy bookshop, a turn-of-the-century Everyman's Library reprint of an 1836 sojourn in Brazil entitled *The Naturalist on the Amazons*. I flicked through it idly, decided that its price of £2 was too much for such a tawdry little thing, and was about to put it back into its few square inches of dusty oblivion when a single word lodged in the corner of an eye and transposed itself into an avalanche of mind-rocks. Where had I heard that word before? Where, dammit? Why did it ring so familiar on my tongue? I bought the book on the whim of that word, and took it home in a fervour of memory-scouring. Over and over again I looked at the word on the page and spoke its familiar syllables until at last the fog of memory cleared and I saw again a shaft of smoky sunlight in a backroom barber's shop. Then I heard the word in a different voice. A voice of someone faking an accent, clipped and smooth, vowels round and southern, a voice speaking not in its accustomed conversational Lancastrian but in a kind of Victorian travelogue. The word it spoke was 'Curupira'. I had stumbled on Grampa's script.

Time has landscaped away Grampa's house, the Astoria cinema which he once managed, and Willie McWalter's shop where he held court. The newest buildings are bright and airy and likeable, but there are only grass banks, trees, shrubs and sunlight where the squalid landmarks of his life once stood, squalid but unfailingly brightened by his irrepressible spirit. It is not hard to understand now why he so loved Rossini overtures. His life was lived with the same chuckling *brio*, and all sombre passages would be brief and swept aside with the inevitable resurgent good humour. Walking his half-mile of Lochee now, it is as though some benevolent champion of his memory has softened the profile of its old dingy canyon and let light into it. The idea pleases me greatly.

A bend in the road, just beyond what I think of as the limit of his territory, wraps round two sides of a small graveyard. I remember it from childhood as a place where I whiled away the occasional summer hour when adult conversation at Grampa's palled. It seemed vaguely exotic at the time, not really a part of my territory, frequented by Lochee lads I rather feared; they wore boots which sparked. Huge trees fringed its small steep acre, a rounded mound with mostly small grey stones. The grass was often long, an uncut informality which added age to the stones and adventure to the games we played there. For such places were playgrounds, not the home of the dead; paradise for hide-and-seekers, or adventurers with Dinkies and toy soldiers, or a calm reservoir of birds and butterflies to one like me whose eye has been in the thrall of nature from the very first.

But to step into its summer embrace now and scan it with a middle-aged eye is to recognise not a playground but a time capsule, an intact period piece where the lives and livelihoods of the first half of nineteenth-century Lochee are cut in tablets of stone. There is no stone older than 1810, none newer than 1855. Many were erected years after the deaths they commemorate. Many specify 'Lochee' after the names and occupations of the dead or the survivors who commissioned the stones. Is there a more self-consciously Lochee place than this?

The occupations speak of a way of life as lost to time as Grampa's landmarks: Flaxdresser, Wright, Weaver, Innkeeper, Mariner, Merchant, Mason, Baker, Coaler, Feuar, Carter, Flourmiller . . . There is one 'Late Gunner in the Royal Navy'. Another, conspicuous by its rarity value, 'Surgeon, Lochee'. There are incomers, seemingly as self-conscious of their origins as the natives: 'Charles Stewart, Gardiner, Blackness' must have emigrated all of a mile-and-a-half, and had his occupation misspelled into the bargain. Another stone misspells Thornton, Rattray and 'their' as Thoronton, Rattery and thire, which somehow makes even more poignant the tribute to 'five of thire children who all died in infancy'.

The names predominate with the blunt monosyllables of the east coast: Cant, Fyfe, Gray, Speed, Sim, Reid, Brown, Flight, Bruce, Young, Doig, Miln, Bell and others as familiar as these on Dundee ears, like Robertson, Rollo, Yeaman. There are few Macs, few other Highland names.

The flowing italicised numerals, '1813' betray the eloquent hand of 'James Stewart, *Mason*' (more italics). He could do Gothic letters, too, and there is no better inscribed lament than his own commemoration of his children aged 3 years 9 months, and 2 years, and his mother. But the other side records *his* death, the words cut by a prosaic and unmoved hand unworthy of the man.

Several stones are two-sided. One dated 1811 begins again on side two thus: 'Revised 1855'.

This is a good place to just sit and not worry about splitting infinitives like that any more than the nineteenth century worried about misspelling a stone. The commemoration is no less. Grampa isn't buried here. No twentieth-century ghost is. Besides, much as he made Lochee his own, his 'Illingworth', much less his 'Timothy' would have sat uncomfortably on this green summer heap. But I can hear him better here than anywhere else.

Somewhere about here, Lochee Road becomes Logie Street, and snakes its way to Lochee High Street, at which point one of the great through routes in and out of Dundee has been thoughtlessly splintered in the bullying name of traffic management. Continuity and that priceless intangible, community, have been butchered. The commercial high ground of Lochee has been sundered from its calmer low ground, the snake's head sundered from its tail. It has become two places, all to accommodate traffic which does not want to stop there. I can still make the connection in my mind between high and low, but only because I am old enough. Younger generations cannot. A crucial thread has been snapped and the place is the poorer for it, and so are its people.

Chapter Seven

The Great Lum

Across the junction from Wooler's bike shop (another ageless survivor which was the hub of my cycling childhood and youth, and the last resting place of precious pocket money and paper-round wages), a slim street as mud-coloured as any Dundee street of pedigree creeps between what were once the walls of jute mills. Beyond the eerily implanted acres of tarmacked open space at the end of the street towers one monumental familiarity. Surely only Dundee, of all the industrial cities on the planet, has a love affair with a lum. Cox's stack is as much a Dundee phenomenon as a Lochee one, for all that its gargantuan roots clasp Lochee soil. Folk all over Dundee know someone who toiled slavishly to make it belch, an inheritance which might have been expected to induce revulsion rather than reverence. But there can have been few more unanimous public outrages in Dundee than the one the natives mustered a few years ago in response to a proposal to demolish it. From every vantage point, and especially from the Hully and the Lah, Cox's stack is as conspicuous as the Bell Rock Lighthouse on its horizon.

So much of what Dundee's built skyline has become these last three or four unflattering decades is just tall junk, and in all that tawdry company, Cox's stack is architecture. It may have been built to foul the city air with the unwanted residue of the jute industry and it may have been brick built in a stone-built city, but it was built beautifully and it survives beautifully, or at least it survives beautifully at a distance. For the junk culture which disfigures Dundee's skyline has also been tellingly at work around the feet of the great lum.

The handsome, mud-coloured walls now house not mills but their aftermaths, their shells. One has acquired smoked glass and Tesco bides in it. The other is flats with a basement carpark. Cars! In a muhll! In their heydays they sucked in and exhaled a dark and bronchial regiment of cobble-sparking feet. Alfie would cite Burns at you, 'out the hellish legion sallied'. But it was baits and bikes that sallied. Alfie'd sigh: 'Ahthin's cheenged'. Between the two great shells (both stone-cleaned now, incongruously demure for such a grime-belching industry) is another carpark of vast acreage, fringed with some of the nastiest red-brick upstarts your eyes ever winced at, red brick decorated with pale brick – trite homage to the overlordship of the great lum. If it was the developer's intention here to defer respectfully or even obliquely to Cox's stack, it has not worked. Only architectural insult has been achieved and the fact that Dundee is over-familiar with these is scant excuse for more.

And then, on a wedge of grass, like the Bell Rock Lighthouse transplanted to Rannoch Moor (and just as useless) stands the lum, attached to nothing. It is a relic, a historic monument, a souvenir of the jute industry . . . no, not a souvenir, *the* souvenir, the only one we ever took to our hearts, the only one we ever spared a second glance. The jute barons were forever gracing (as they saw it) their mill buildings with facades and ornaments, symbols of their own self-importance, though some of them survive now as distinguished if faintly preposterous architecture. The Cox brothers were the only ones to lavish their egos on a lum, a curious affectation in a city awash with lums in the nineteenth century, but a lum which would proclaim that here was world-wide supereminence of jute. No one thought bigger or dealt or traded bigger than the Cox brothers. The Camperdown works just off Lochee High Street was the biggest and the grandest jute enterprise in the world, and its badge was a lum. It was the symbol of vast fortune. It was the headstone to thousands of Dundonians whose lives were shortened by that gaunt industrial monoculture. Mostly though, it survives now in our affections because time has made it worthy, imparted dignity to its familiarity. To all of us (and including the few who still survive, having slaved in its shadow) no matter how often we clap eyes on it, Cox's stack is a friend, but a friend best greeted from a distance.

We were taught two things about it at the Anky which endure, lodged in my mind because what we were taught there was well taught. One was that it is 282 feet high (and let's not corrupt memory by translating that into metres – it belongs exclusively to its own imperial past). The other was that the balcony at the top is wide enough to drive a horse and cart round it, and some stoorie, cobwebby corner of memory recalls an illustration in a long-forgotten textbook, the horse advancing fearfully among confident passing gulls. For months afterwards, my primary school mind wrestled with the logistics of putting a horse and cart on to that airy promenade.

Cox's stack still exercises the mind. Whose idea was its colossal scope: jute baron's or architect's? Given that it was built in an era (the 1860s) when Dundee cultivated factory lums the way the Forestry Commission has since sprouted sitka spruces, and folk with nothing better to do could count 150 from the Tap o the Lah, why was so much care and architectural class lavished on it? Did the Coxes really have nothing more than baronial one-upmanship in mind? Or were they thinking beyond the inevitable demise of their era? Was this remarkable incursion into Dundee's jute-fouled air a gesture towards posterity, a permanent milestone to chart Dundee's industrial journey, so that folk like me can look on the lum's fair face and have it represent the city that lies just out of sight over memory's shoulder?

Whatever the motivation, the thing harks back to a time when brickies built with vision, and what they constructed was as much art as function. And the one function that none could have forseen then, is that now its presence on the landscape of the city, from whatever distance you view it, clasps Dundee and Lochee together, and amen to that, I say.

Cox's stack has one more claim to fame, and not even the Cox family could ever have imagined that posterity would honour their endeavours in quite such an eccentric manner as the city of Dundee concocted in 1995. To mark the regeneration of the city centre, the city commissioned three small sculptures, each no more than a couple of feet high, and set on eye-level plinths just across from the City Square. The Princess of Wales unveiled the Royal Arch (a Victorian monster which used to lord it blackly over the entrance to the docks, happily long demolished, but unquestionably a vast city landmark for generations); the Wishart Arch in the Cowgate, probably the oldest surviving built stone in Dundee after the Old Steeple; and . . . not the Old Steeple itself which is *the* great city centre landmark, not even the Pillars which is everyone's favourite symbol of demolished Dundee, but Cox's Stack. A sculpture of an undemolished chimney! A monument to a lum! Every time I pass it now, I give it a pat, and think myself fortunate that this ahld hame toon o mine is still capable of such sublime pointlessness. It's a crucial part of what being a Dundonian is all about. I love it.

Chapter Eight

The Road and the Miles

Dundee has long been clasped to larger spheres of influence than Lochee, of course. Time was when the postal address was 'Dundee, Angus'. Most of us regret the demise of that official coupling. In practice it has always been that way. Who bides in Dundee who does not claim to be a son or a daughter of Angus's rust-red earth? Who bides in Auchmithie or Inverarity or Carnoustie or Kirrie who does not trade with or trade on the proximity of Dundee and its occasional fame and infamy? We trespass mutually when it suits us. All manner of ties bind us.

Dundee is a hub from which spokes of traipsing humanity have radiated for a thousand years. In my portion of that span, the traipsing was for the berries, the tatties, the hulls, bike runs in the seeven weekies, and for the hell of it. James McIntosh Patrick – forever Mahcky Pat hereabouts, and Dundee's definition of art – traipses the spokes to paint, making the landscapes of such as Kinnordy and Sidlaw, Auchterhouse and Lundie as famous as himself. Gillie, of course, travelled that one spoke in particular from Coupar Angus, to claim immortality. Now, more than thirty years after the event that was his explosive arrival in our midst, the Dundee F.C. fanzine calls itself *Eh Mind o Gillie*, the title taken from the . . . ah . . . poem which adorns the back page.

For glory days I often pine
All those great times once enjoyed,
The famous Dundee half-back line
Of Gallacher, Cowie and Boyd,
The golden moments I still recall,
Steeling down the wing went Billy,
But, without doubt, the best of all
Is when Eh mind o Gillie.

Thus is immortality conferred. Where were we? Ah yes, the radiating spokes. The Broons are aye trauchlin oot tae the but 'n' ben yet, and smokies still make it into Dundee fish shops or to the 'schemes' in wee vans from Arbroath; a sublime edge-of-the-pavement scent to rival Braithwaite's coffee shop (Dundee's aesthetic foundation stone, an exotic scent which made Bisto Kids of us all, enlivening even the drabbest day with potent and tangible hints of the finer things in life).

Besides all that, we all have cousins in Wellbank and aunties in Arbroath or Brechin. My father, having lost his parents as a child, was brought up by his mother's sister from somewhere up Forfar way, and that bloodline put Anderson branches on the family tree and Angus soil under our feet, and established Auntie Meg as a seminal figure in the lives of all the family. She was a matriarch, a survivor from an earlier era, a stoic designed specifically by some perverse God to accommodate all the world's ills in a single burden and bear it with Shylock's patient shrug, for sufferance is the badge of all her tribe, too. She commanded awe and love in more or less equal measure, disapproved of the world more or less entirely, laughed more or less silently (a quiet hiss would escape from her lips while her shoulders moved gently up and down – it was all the pleasure I ever remember emanating from her). She was tall and slender and, in later life at least, she grew slow and stooped; old mother time.

She loved my father as if he were her own son. She was in her eighties and in hospital when she was told that Dad had died in the same hospital from cancer. She gave up living at that point, became merely mortal in my eyes and, finally deprived of the one great reason she had left for staying alive, she died. She will resurrect soon in this account, for in the story of Dundee as I know it, she was the ultimate one-way spoke-traveller. The death of her sister in the winter of 1918 left her life without choice. She went south because it was required of her, south from that Angus which was all she had ever known of the world, uprooted from the rust-red earth for the mud-grey tenement walls, a spinster earmarked by circumstance to subjugate herself to the needs of her dead sister's six children. If she ever looked back in regret, she did so in silence and alone. She did not fail her sister, nor the demands of the burden.

Faither would reclaim his Angus inheritance when, after his Army days (Royal Horse, Eighth Army, Desert Rats with Monty, Dunkirk, El Alamein, God knows where else, Berlin at the end – he had a full and adventurous war, emerging as unscathed as anyone could), he became a Post Office telephone engineer. It was a couthier Post Office then which managed phones from wee green vans with ladders on the top. Dad's patch for many years made an inveterate spoke-traveller of him, for it was bounded by Dundee in the south, Bridge of Cally in the north-west and the sea in the east. In that perpetual exposure to the countryside of Angus and east Perthshire was born – or at least awakened – a love-by-osmosis of hill and mountain country which he only ever articulated by way of his own all-purpose slogan of profound approval: 'Ah, the bonnie hulls.'

What I inherited in turn was a refined and more ancient form of the same landscape love, some dark survival, and – forbye the Hully – I probably owe the seed of it to Auntie Meg and the Post Office and wee green vans like GUL 569 and OYF 105 that smelled of cables and tools and mysterious leather boxes and weird contraptions which helped a man to squirrel up a telegraph pole; vans that brought the red earth home to Dundee on their tyres. We never had a TV set until I was fifteen, but I was fluent on the phone at the age of seven, which was rare in 1954.

The spoke-travellers had their anthem. Dundee has always liked to sing, and what it likes to sing about best is itself. 'Out of the strong came forth sweetness' as they say on kitchen table syrup tins, for Dundee's song-sweetness comes out of strong things – industry, labour, ships, stone places, folk. The ballad repertoire is as rich as it is robust, and Angus reciprocates with songs of farm things, of fatherless bairns up Noran Water, and geese on the wing. At the core of their joint repertoire are a handful of songs which travel well and have been sung all across the world by folk who have never clapped eyes on us. Fair enough. You don't have to be a Finn to love Sibelius.

But the great enigma of the collection, its subtle masterpiece, is a wistful boy-meets-girl story, tantalisingly understated and incomplete, mysterious for all its familiarity. I grew up singing 'The Road and the Miles to Dundee' because everyone in Dundee grew up singing it. I've sung it in Shetland and Skye and Newtonmore and Donside and the Borders and Lancaster, to name but a few, and never yet encountered fellow carousers who were unfamiliar with it. But then I started not just to sing it but think about it. No other song I know poses and fails to answer so many questions.

> Cold winter was howling o'er moor and o'er mountain
> And wild was the surge of the dark rolling sea,
> When just about daybreak I met a young lassie
> Who asked me the road and the miles to Dundee.

So, a young woman is alone and apparently lost, and trying to get to Dundee, alone and at daybreak in the worst of winter weather. Why is she there, what is the purpose of her journey, and why travelling alone?

> Said I to the lassie, 'I canna weel tell ye
> The road and the distance I canna weel gie,
> But gin ye'll permit me tae gang a wee bittie
> I'll show ye the road and the miles to Dundee.

So the singer/narrator is also on the road, and whatever his purpose in such foul weather, he is not averse to abandoning it to escort the young lassie. You can almost see his mind at work: he tells her he is not certain of the distance, and perhaps his directions would be confusing, but he is willing to escort her part of the way – well, it's better than anything he had planned for the day.

> At once she consented and gie'd me her airm
> Not a word did I spier wha the lassie micht be;
> She appeared like an angel in feature and form
> As she walked by my side on the road to Dundee.

86

So she is both beautiful and well dressed (you don't get scruffy angels) and desperate enough to accept the offer of escort from a stranger. But why, oh why does he decline to ask her who she is? Tongue tied and shy? Well, not too shy to offer to escort her!

> At length wi the Howe o Strathmartine behind us
> The spires o the toon in full view we could see,
> She said, 'Gentle sir, I ne'er will forget ye
> For showing me so far on the road to Dundee.'

So they crossed the Howe of Strathmartine, which puts geography on their route. And he has brought her as far as some high ground where Dundee is visible, which is hardly what he set out to do, to 'gang a wee bittie, and show ye the road . . . '

Now the song begins to disagree with itself, for there are two versions of the denouement. One, the more common one, says this:

> She took the gowd pin from the scarf on her bosom
> And said, 'Take ye this in remembrance o me,'
> Then bravely I kissed the sweet lips o the lassie
> E'er I parted wi her on the road tae Dundee

Fair enough, although a gold pin seems an excessive gift under the circumstances, unless the lassie's plight was truly desperate. But the other version inserts an extra verse, puts the gowd pin on the man's 'bosom' and invokes an exchange of gifts:

> 'This ring and this purse take to prove I am grateful
> And some simple token I trust ye'll gie me,
> So in times to come I'll remember the laddie ,
> Who showed me the road and the miles to Dundee.'

> I took the gowd pin that I wear at my bosom
> And said, 'Keep ye this in remembrance o me,'
> Then bravely I kissed the sweet lips o the lassie
> Ere I parted wi her on the road to Dundee.

A ring *and* a purse? And she asks for a token in return, so clearly – or rather implicitly, for nothing is clear about the song's story – they have established enough of a rapport *en route* to want to commemorate the encounter. Yet still she has not volunteered and he has not asked about her and her journey, but there is an exchange of gifts and the one kiss, on the lips, if you please. Then there is this:

So here's to the lassie, I ne'er will forget her
And ilka young laddie wha's listening to me—
Oh never be sweir tae convoy a young lassie
Though it's only tae show her the road to Dundee.

No hint of regret, no sign that anything was on his mind other than the gentleman's cause of assisting a damsel in distress. And his trophies are enough – the purse, the ring, the kiss and the memory which he took home, back the way he came (which you now suspect he knew all along) alone to his home on the moor between mountain and sea.

But it is the lassie who is the song's enigma. What happened to her? Did she go on alone to Dundee having been escorted until the spires of the toon came into view? What fate awaited her there? Did she forget her escort at once, or did she ever keep a piece of her heart aside for him caught in a locket of time, his gold pin on her bosom? And who was she? Journeys to Dundee or through Angus are forever putting her in my mind. You tend to catch yourself humming a snatch of it whenever the landscape fits, the way you sing the 'Skye Boat Song' to yourself on the ferry.

The writer in me began to search for storylines which might explain away the song. A solution, when I eventually found it, emerged from the one place I had never thought to look, until one winter's day up the Hully, I was brushing away the moss and lichen from the lettering on my grandmother's long-neglected grave and read:

A token of respect from a few friends
In loving memory of Jane Crumley
who died 20th December, 1918

The thought stuck in my mind . . . 'Five days before Christmas, six children effectively orphaned; that must have been some winter for them . . .'

The year of our Lord, nineteen hundred and eighteen. The dead of winter, the iron hard dead, the winter stillness of grey ice, the vice stillness of shuddering cold, the moor both wan and dark, the mountains in the west a shrug lost to the snow-grey encampment of low-hung winter sky, the sea licking and listless in the east. I know this cold, this winter deadness. It is my life's one adversary. My father, if he taught me anything at all, taught me to respect it. So I meet the dead of winter head on. I tackle it on its own terms. I grow iron hard myself, I let the grey ice touch my heart, so that in this living-dead hour of Nature I maintain a kinship with the land to which I am yoked. The cold is the land's adversary too. Together the land and I grow quiet as winter, we make the same respectful pause as Nature, subdued as hedgehogs.

He taught me also, my father, to keep a weather eye on the sea, that distant visible sea, that fickle manipulator. I fear the sea and travel it with the greatest reluctance. My grandfather and his father and his were whalers out of Dundee. The sea buried them all. Mercifully, my own father put a stop to that salted rot and put his own dour faith in the land. This high shelf of moor was his small legacy to me, that and this low and dull-red house, alone as I am myself on its plinth of moor. Here I was born, here I grew up, here I watched my parents die, here I live and here I work the land, keeping a patch of the moor green.

For ten days the ice-stillness had been on the land. Now it was the eleventh and the wind was risen hugely in the north-east. There was snow in its fist. The sea heaved and whitened. I had been out checking the beasts in the parks. There was a figure on the road, a woman. In white.

And I am the Singer of the Song.

There is a figure on the road, a man in black on a bike. His knock chills, chills as no winter cold ever could. We thole winter cold well enough here. It is a part of us, part of our condition, part of our land's sea station, part of the proximity of the mountains. But that knock is a deeper chill. My heart is gripped by it.

'Meg, get the door, lass, why don't you. The man'll catch es daith if you leave him standing there much longer.'

'Aye, Faither, I'm goin, I'm goin.'

Aye, daith. There's daith in that knock.

'Mistress Anderson?'

'Aye.'

'A telegram for you, lass.'

'A *telegram?*'

'What isst, Meg?' Faither's voice from ben.

'A telegram.'

'A *telegram?*

'Well bring the mannie and es telegram in and shut the cahld oot. We dinnae wahnt the fire to be heatin the hale o Angus.'

'Aye, Faither.'

I brought the mannie in. He had cycled from Forfar with the thing. That meant it was urgent. That meant, as far as fowk like oorsels were concerned, a daith. Faither and I looked at the stupid thing in my hand and shared the same black foreboding.

I had never seen a telegram before, didn't know how to open it. Faither looked at it, helpless with apprehension. The mannie suggested a knife to slit it open. Then he handed it back wordlessly and we read its curious language together, Faither and I:

REGRET SISTER JANE DEAD PNEUMONIA STOP CHILDREN
EFFECTIVELY ORPHANED AS FATHER'S WHEREABOUTS UNKNOWN
STOP CAN YOU HELP STOP DOCTOR JAMES PURDIE DUNDEE
ROYAL INFIRMARY

It had never occurred to me before that there should be a 'p' at the start of pneumonia. I couldn't see any reason for it now.

And I am the Lassie of the Song.

Few enough folk walk the road by the farm. Tinkers looking for a free meal or a drink. Tramps looking for a corner of a barn for a bed, men down on their luck mostly. I count my blessings and put them up. But a woman alone? I couldna remember such a thing in all my thirty years. I walked down the track to meet her. It was just getting light so she must have been on the road in the dark. It was a queer thing, this.

When she spoke, the voice was steady, unalarmed, an Angus country voice like my own, a touch further to the north and the east, more the sea of it than the mountain and moor of it. She had lost her way in the dark and the weather. Could I tell her the road – 'and the miles', she asked as an afterthought – to Dundee?

'Dundee! Fae here, Lassie?' I thought how I might explain the tortuous way down to the main road south. In this weather and the half-light it would take her hours. Yet – here was another queerness – she seemed quite untouched by either the weather or her predicament. She was cool and controlled. Just lost.

The thing to do, I offered, was to escort her, not to the main road but across the old hill road grown green again through disuse and down to the Howe of Strathmartine. From the high ground to the south of the Howe she would see the town and I could point her the way and leave her to it – whatever 'it' might be, whatever purpose was behind her journeying. I proposed the plan, tentatively. She accepted at once, gratefully but with no smile. I took her arm and we set off.

And I am the Singer of the Song.

So it was decided. Faither had put his foot down and stamped heavily on my protests. Dundee: it would suffocate me! Nothing of the kind, Meg, he had said. It's ah sea wunds. And for all the sharn in the streets there's aye the Tay, and the toon's twa hulls are as blithe as the Clovy. Well, we both knew that wasn't true, for we held Glen Clova as something like Holy Ground. Moses on his Sinai went no more respectfully than when Faither and I (and Mither when she was aboot) climbed up the Clovy. What aboot *you*, Faither, I had protested, straw-clutching now, for I kenned fine what aboot Faither. I'll no leave ye alone, I telt him. I've only been alone once in my life he said, on Flanders Field wi a bullet in my leg, then a German soldier found me, gave me a fag and said 'Your friends are coming for you, never fear comrade.' No I won't be alone, Meg.

Besides, I'm ahld, he said. Jane's six bairns are – what – atween fower an twel? They need *someone*. You're ah that's left.

Then he gave me two things. A purse that was my mother's, though whether there was so much as a pound in it, I never found out. And a ring that was her mother's, though what I might do with either of them was beyond me. I had a purse, I could aye hawk the ring. I suppose, for it looked gowd enough to me.

I rose in the deep dark of the winter morning, 4 a.m. I had not slept. I could not thole the parting wi Faither, so I was up and out and away at that blackest hour and not even the howl of winter's worst across the moor and into the mountains could deter me, and God knows what fears were accruing among the boats on such a wild sea. So I dressed in the bonniest claes I had, which were cream and silken, thinking I would find nae cheerfu moment the rest o my life after I reached that ahld grey toon. If the road and the miles to Dundee were to be the last free hours of my life, then here's tae them, and I'll go bonny and damn that God and his winter. For what man'll spare me sae muckle's a sideweys glance after I've given my best years tae six bairns he didnae sire?

It was but a twa-three mile to the main road, but I little kenned the way. The farm and the lane to the village were ah my world, and the way up the burn to the hills. By daybreak I had to acknowledge that I was worse than unfamiliar wi the grund. I was lost. But it was a sea wind, so as long as I held my left side to it, I would be heading south at least. Then, there was a lit doorway up a track and a concerned voice nearby.

And I am the Lassie of the Song.

So the morning grew and the weather wearied of itself and went quiet and iron-cold again as we walked side by side. Here and there she took my arm where the going was roughest. At each linking, she put a quiet smile on me. An angel in feature and form! So finely dressed, too, and she neither tired nor dishevelled her dress nor suffered the winter cold. She walked as if the wild winter was not a part of the day. An angel, I thought it again and again as I stole gleg-eed glances at the lass by my side. If there's such a thing as angels, this is what they look like.

Chae waved to me from the inn, beckoned me over for a glass

of beer. No the day, Chae, but maybe on the wey hame.

We walked on, down into the Howe wi'oot words. Queer, thinkin back now, but I spiered not a word about who the lassie might be, nor what might be the purpose on the road, nor why, though the winter assailed me to my bones, she appeared to cleave through it ah, unperturbed as a warm knife in a pat o butter. She wore a shield unseen and benevolent to wrap her, to safeguard her journey, to fulfil her purpose, or so it seemed to me, and if that doesn't sound like the travels of an angel, what does?

And I am the Singer of the Song.

At length, with what I now know to be the Howe o Strathmartine behind us (though I never knew of the cunning hill track he led me down) we topped a small rise and saw the spires and reekin lums of Dundee in full view. At that moment I knew relief, gratitude and despair in equal measure. I stood on the threshold of that other life, a dark life of bairns I hadna borne. Jane's bairns. Wha kens, I told myself, if I'll ever see this Howe, they hills, the peesie-loud parks o Faither's farm at Inverarity, Faither esel . . . any of it, ever again? For sure, I'll no see this laddie, this braw escort o mine (for he was braw!) ever again. How could I tell *him* o my fate? *Why* should I deave him owre ah that? Doubtless he has sorrows tae thole esel wi'oot shoulderin *my* burden.

Yet would he no be the last braw man in my life? I had somehow to mark the hour, even if it wis only a wey o fuellin future dreams. Then I saw he wore a gowd pin shaped like a swan at the scarf that happit his bosom. I couldna ask him for that, no outright, and what could I offer him in return . . . except . . .

'Tak this purse an this ring, sir,' I told him . . . 'my gratitude . . . and . . . perhaps there is some simple token you can gie me so that in times to come I'll remember the lad who showed me the road and the miles to Dundee?' These were my words to him.

And I am the Lassie of the Song.

A purse and a gold ring! Whatever was in the purse (and I darena open it in her presence) it was more than I had expected – for I had expected nothing at all when I offered to convoy the lass down the Dundee road. But what could I give her? On the spur of the moment

I snatched the swan brooch off the scarf that I wore in winters, that brooch that was my mother's. Her barely concealed sadness might know the buoyancy of swan wings. Remember me by swan wings, I told her. Then, on another impulse (and two in one day is a wheen of impulses for an Angus farm chiel) and knowing that we'd bide in different worlds forever and never meet again, I kissed her lips, just brushed them wi mine, an they were sweet as ripe pears and I loved her then and forever. I turned north back down into the Howe and she turned south where her city and her fate awaited her.

In the inn on the edge of the moor, I found Chae at it still, and in red-cheeked good humour.

'You ta'en yer time, man,' he bellowed.

'I had tae convoy the young lassie ye seen me wi . . . '

'Lassie? What wey would you hae a lass tae convoy?'

'You saw her, Chae, when ye beckoned me owre this moarnin. That lassie.'

Chae frowned.

'Jimmy,' he told me carefully, awful careful with his words suddenly, 'I agree I've hed a gless or twa the day, but I mind the moarnin fine. I mind the moarnin, I mind wavin ye owre, but Jimmy lad, ye were on yer ain. There wisnae a lassie. Thir wis nae a lassie.'

'Havers, man, and here's my toast til er. Now here's tae the lassie. I'll never forget her, and abdy that's listenin tae's – never be sweir tae convoy a young lassie, though it's only tae show her doon the road tae Dundee!' I drank to her. But Chae would have none of it.

'Jimmy. Ye were on yer ain.'

'Look, Chae, I'll show ye. She gie'd me her purse an her ring.'

So I put my hand in my pocket to produce the purse and the gold ring but all that my fingers closed on was the familiar shape of my own wee swan brooch that was my mother's.

And I am the Singer of the Song, and my song is sung.

These last few years it has been a spoke to and from the west I have travelled, to and from Dundee that is the hub of my life still, wherever I might wash up. I come along the river, past the *Discovery* and the docks to the Ferry. There is a shingle shore there where I often walk to see the city on its low wide shore of the Firth. There, too, a single swan is apt to detach itself from a resident and fluctuating group and step ashore. She steps tall and slim, she dresses in creamy white, like an angel in feature and form.

Chapter Nine

The Goalie

Bette Crumley's eyes widened at the sight of me on her doorstep. Then they relaxed into a smile. She would tell me later: 'When Eh opened the door and saw you standing there, Eh could hardly believe meh eyes. It was like going back, oh, so many years. You're so like the Crumleys!'

At that same moment, when she opened the door to find me waiting, and I saw her, a small woman with a vividly alert face, a shining-white-haired almost octogenarian, I also saw a man step into the light at the far end of the lobby. Her husband Douglas stood there. I could hardly believe my eyes. It was like going back, oh, so many years. He was so like the Crumleys!

'Hello, stranger,' he greeted me, and the eyes that were the source of the smile were eyes I have known all my life. But I am 48-years-old as I write this and Doug Crumley is 81, and I have just learned of his existence. Forty-eight is old to learn that for all of your life you have been regularly passing within a few hundred yards of the home of an uncle you never knew you had. In my parents' time, ours was a close family. We were forever visiting relatives or being visited by them. Why not this one?

And anyway, what am I doing here now, widening the eyes of

Bette with my throwback features, deaving the pair of them with questions?

My book, and for that matter my life, had hit a stumbling block. Books take over this writer's life to an absurd extent when they are being written. When the subject of the book impinges so directly on the writer's life for its raw material, there are few waking hours not absorbed in the process of scouring the mind for straws to clutch, and there are more waking hours than normal. So the book and I duly stumbled and, having stumbled, I picked up what it was we had both stumbled over and I studied it. It measured $2\frac{1}{2}$ inches by $1\frac{1}{4}$, or 6.5 cm by 3.5 cm if you must. It was a cigarette card, with a black-and-white photograph on the front – a young man with impeccably parted hair, a robust and familiar chin (familiar from my father, his brother, his uncle, and from the bathroom mirror), arms folded across a wide-collared shirt. The caption, white lettering on a black surround, said simply:

R. Crumley,
Dundee F.C.

On the back of the card there was:

Smith's
CUP TIE
cigarettes
No. 85.

R. Crumley.
Dundee

A very safe goalkeeper who came from Newcastle United to his present club.

In packets of 10

My grandfather, Bob Crumley, the cup-winner, the local hero, the goalie. The cigarette card is the only clear picture of him I know of. It was tracked down in Aberdeen by my mother, who thought I might like it. You would think that a man who was once famous in his home town and never left it after he had won his fame would also be easy to track down. But his era was easily scandalised and unforgiving when it came to nursing a grudge. Whatever the nature of the wedge driven between Bob Crumley and his young family of six children, and whatever the pain and bitterness it engendered, it was smothered long since in a pact of silence, or even ignorance, for they were all still children when their mother died and their father was removed from their lives. As they grew up, they had covered my grandfather's traces with silence and distance. I was permitted to know his fame but not his infamy (what was unspoken implied there *was* infamy) nothing of what happened to him, nothing of where or when or how he lived and died.

Was he still alive when I was a child, as my other grandfather was?

Could I have walked past him in the street not knowing he was my grandfather? He not knowing his own grandson? Did he die knowing nothing at all of all fourteen of his grandchildren?

The more I thought about him, about his perpetual presence in the shadows of family life, the more portent a force he became, the more so because ours was a family apparently free from shadows. As a child I had traded unashamedly on his name in any footballing company. At school, several of my teachers were intrigued to find two of his descendants in their midst. And at D.C. Thomson's, his name helped me on my journalistic way and even got me into football grounds free when several editors decided early on that I was football reporting material, and who was I to complain about such a fate?

And always, the denial of Bob Crumley's life by his own family added mystique to the potency. If I was to write about Dundee through my own eyes, I would not deny him.

Besides, I believe now that my father and his brothers and sisters could have had their code of silence imposed on them by two seminal figures in their lives, Auntie Meg (their dead mother's sister) who brought them up, and Uncle Jim (Bob Crumley's brother), who was a persuasive, powerful and loving influence on my father throughout his life. I have before me the letter of condolence he wrote to my mother after Dad died, the very handwriting betraying the grief of an old man mourning someone he regarded almost as his own son. But whatever the enjoinment the family elders may have wished upon Dad's generation, I felt unconstrained by it.

Bob Crumley was a name the city knew well and, mostly,

admired. Remarkably, considering he has been dead almost fifty years and his footballing exploits occurred more than eighty years ago, he is remembered still. But my father was as principled a man as I ever met, and he did not share in the admiration. Something put ill-feeling and unbridgeable distance between him and the man who had been his father. I think often of how much I loved and admired my father when he was alive, of the unspoken bond between us, of how much I have mourned him and missed him in the twenty years since he died, of how often I have invoked his memory in some shape or form in moments of crisis or celebration or quiet conversation, of how he crops up in dreams and daydreams. And the more all that goes on, the more profound is my sorrow that my own father was denied this thing of such value, or that he denied it himself.

Bob Crumley, the man, was not a permitted topic of conversation. Bob Crumley, the goalie, was broachable, and it may be that Dad respected his niche in Dundee's sporting annals, for he loved many sports and respected excellence in all of them. His father had achieved a kind of local sporting immortality and (in my hearing at least) he never attempted to belittle that achievement. But Bob Crumley, the man, was under wraps. I wonder now how much my father ever knew him. He was only three when World War I erupted so Bob Crumley was absent for the next four years, and he must have been a bewildered little seven-year-old by the time the war ended, his mother dead, and his father returned bearing the inevitable burden of that hideous conflict. But Dad died too young for me to have grown old enough to ask him these things.

Bob Crumley is the missing name from that roll call of my family interred 'up the Hully' among the worms and the blahckies. What there is, however, is that tiny and somehow piteous stone dated and inscribed 20 December 1918 to Jane Crumley, his wife, my grandmother, 'a token of respect from a few friends'. It is all the commemoration there is.

There were moments while my father was still alive that my mother covertly hinted at the darkness which lived on in Dad's mind. There was even a suggestion, and my mother was the source of that, too, that Bob Crumley was buried in a pauper's grave, and that that was also up the Hully. I wrestled too often for comfort with the idea that my father would never have permitted such a thing, despite all that had gone before. But years after Dad had died, Mum would talk about it all more openly, and in so doing, revealed how little she really knew of those two torn generations of the family she had married. Now that she too is dead, I have felt something grow in me, a kind of spiritual commandment, to attempt a healing.

I want to approach my grandfather's grave in a spirit of reconciliation. I want to advance through the bliss of my ignorance and say:

'This has gone on long enough. It's over.'

But first, I must find my grandfather's grave.

And if the family had borne away all that they knew to graves of their own, perhaps there was a pool of knowledge to be tapped among strangers with long memories and a spirit of generosity. It is no idle boast to say that I know Dundee to be well endowed with both. I did the only thing a former journalist with Dundee beginnings could do in the circumstances. I wrote to the *Courier*, where my whole writer's adventure began. Two former colleagues (from longer ago than any of us would care to remember), Irene Rowe and Angela Mathers, gave me a very sympathetic hearing, contrived a generous article in the paper's daily Craigie column headed 'Seeking information about his footballer grandfather', printed a follow-up article the following day in response to the first two phone calls, and promised to send on all subsequent information received. I quote the first two paragraphs of the follow-up articles:

> The query about former goalkeeper Bob Crumley drew a speedy response from Mr Cavanagh of Dundee. He recalls that Mr Crumley lived across the road from him in Benvie Road, Dundee, during the war years, by which time he was 'an old man with a bunnet'.
>
> According to Mr Cavanagh, he would come out on nights and sit on the window ledge while children were playing football. 'We knew he was in the 1910 cup-winning side,' he said, 'but he wasn't very approachable. I think he was totally blind by then.'

Blind?

There had never been any mention of Bob Crumley going blind. I suddenly wondered if my father had even known. I thought back again to that solitary meeting which Mum had told me about when Dad pointed out Bob Crumley to her across the street. There was no mention of his blindness then, in the late 1930s. Now I thought of him old and blind and 'unapproachable', and living no more than a 20-minute walk away from any address my parents stayed in for all the years he might have lived. It suddenly seemed more wrong than I had ever imagined it could have been. I would never condemn my parents. They were among the most hospitable, compassionate and principled people I have ever known. The irresistible conclusion then is that they lived constrained and in ignorance. Either that or they breached the constraint in secrecy. I have no way of knowing. Then the phone rang, to announce the existence of Douglas and Bette Crumley. They had seen the *Courier* article about the man Doug Crumley called 'Uncle Bob'.

Uncle Bob? Then who . . . ?

'There were three brothers,' Doug Crumley explained. 'There was your grandfather, there was Uncle Jim, and there was my father – Will Crumley.'

Will Crumley? A *third* brother? There was never a mention of a Will Crumley, not once in all the countless conversations about the Crumley family that I had sat through or eavesdropped on or initiated. Not once.

So that was how I found myself on the doorstep of a trim little flat off the Arbroath Road, built on the site, if you please, of the football pitch where a side called Our Boys F.C. played their home games. Our Boys and East End amalgamated in 1893 to become Dundee Football Club. And you wonder at the passion for football which courses through the family bloodline!

And now there was another conundrum. It seems that Will Crumley's wife, Jean, took a right scunner at Uncle Jim. (Bette explained, she being more of an instinctive archivist than Doug. 'Eh'm no a Crumley uv coorse, Eh jist joined up to improve the strain.') She wouldn't let him into the house, wouldn't talk to him, wouldn't acknowledge his existence. Why? Who knows? The conspiracy of silence again. Could it be that Uncle Jim's response to whatever it was had been to freeze out Will and his family. There are times, raking over the embers of this tribe of mine that I feel like the white sheep of the family. Doug and Bette had even been to London to see Uncle Jim (he was long domiciled in the Sooth) and found him 'cold, a bit stand-offish'. I tried to reconcile this view of him with the wholly charming, warm, generous, confiding, wise-cracking, yarn-spinning party-throwing patriarch who turned up in our familial midst from time to time, and the so obvious love and affection which swam to and from him. And when I caught sight of Doug Crumley for the first time, what I saw was Uncle Jim's reincarnation, and I wondered, not for the first time, how my grandfather's generation of the family had so painstakingly warred within itself to such futile ends.

There is also this. I had been led to believe that my grandfather was the villain of the piece, the despoiler of his family, the rash forsaker of his own children. I have tried hard to pin down the source of the information and I cannot, vague memories and dropped hints (some doubtless overheard) among the older members of the family – parents, uncles, aunts, and their contemporaries. But when Doug Crumley began to talk about him, there was no suggestion of that dark side of the man. Instead, there is the child of seven or eight hero-worshipping his Uncle Bob, basking in his reflected glory to the blatant envy of his pals, indulged to the extent that he capered around the Tannadice pitch while Bob Crumley worked as a groundsman – for that is what became of him after his playing days ended at Dens Park. It is tempting to think that one member of the playing staff at Tannadice had a hand in that groundsman's appointment. The Dundee Hibs (later United) goalkeeper was one Jim Crumley – his brother. But in 1921 Jim Crumley was transferred to Swansea, and a crucial distance set in from which the damage to that generation's family infrastructure was irreversible, reconciliation unachievable.

The young Doug Crumley was aware of none of that, and if his Uncle Bob was enshrouded in personal crisis, it didn't show. He remembers 'a cheery kind of chap' who came up for Sunday lunch once a month. Occasionally there were visits to his house in Lochee High Street where he lived alone, then he remarried and came visiting with 'Auntie Jess'. And then, in Doug Crumley's words 'he just disappeared from my life'. The date was 1925, and he was eleven years old.

But there was one extraordinary last meeting, twenty years later, at Tannadice, just after Doug came home from the war. Our conversation went like this:

'After a couple of nights I went up to Tannadice and I saw Uncle

Bob in the enclosure, commentating for the blind lads. So I waited till half-time and went across, didn't speak, and listened to him. He was telling them more about the match than what I could see!'

'He was blind by this time?'

'He was completely blind. He had no eyes. They took them out. I don't know what was wrong. I was just told "Uncle Bob's blind". Anyway, I went across then and said "Hello, Uncle Bob." "Oh! I'm glad to see you got home alright!"'

That was Bob Crumley's instant response to his nephew's voice, and the word 'see' obviously still touches Doug Crumley at the remembrance of it.

'Then I never saw him again.'

There were other replies to the *Courier* article, two from people who knew him as children when he was an old man, one from a relative of his second wife, who had kept a newspaper report of his death and quoted a few of its details. These put tantalising glimpses in my path, and scraps of useful information, particularly his last address at 4 Benvie Road and – crucially – the date of his death. Armed with that, a £10 fee bought me a death certificate, and with three different assurances that he was buried in the Balgay cemetery, I was suddenly close to finding the gravestone that has begun to assume a talismanic significance in my exploration of my home town and my life in it.

I now knew exactly what I wanted to do, privately and alone. Somewhere on that slope of the Hully which faces the afternoon sun sprawled metalically across Invergowrie Bay, there would be a stone with my grandfather's name on it. My parents and my four grandparents earth-to-earth on the same piece of Dundee hillside. I would tell the grave of Bob Crumley that whatever there had been, whatever the distance that had intervened, it was long over, and I was closing the distance, I was healing the old wounds. And what futility was such a wound when all that was sundered was bound again by that single hillside? I wanted to tell the presence at that grave that if torment lingered, I was a broker of peace. More than anything, that is what I wanted to do.

The day was October boisterous, big winds, dazzling river-sun, fast showers, the first autumn fires on the big trees, and twenty years to the day since we had buried Dad here, a barely credible coincidence, as unplanned as it was sublimely appropriate. But I could not find the stone. Eventually, I found a parks department van and asked the driver for help. He did all he could which was to direct me to the department's headquarters across the town where I could have the death certificate checked against a lair number. I left reluctantly, the pilgrim-zeal of the moment stifled.

'At least you have a date,' said a second official. 'We get people in here who are twenty years out.' And he leafed through huge volumes of hand-written names but none of them said Robert Walker Crumley, and he lifted his head and said:

'Well, he certainly isn't buried in the Balgay,' and he patiently leafed through the other main cemetery files while I stood in a small and thoughtless vestibule in a mean red-brick building, surrounded by leaflets and brochures proclaiming the glories of Dundee's parks, while a garish poster incongruously proclaimed the tourist wares of somewhere in Virginia, and both I and my naive, ridiculous and solitary mission stood mutely in shreds. The official came back and shook his head. 'Either he is buried in a churchyard, in which case you have a very difficult search on your hands, or, are you sure he wasn't cremated?'

Not now, I wasn't, because I had been sure he was buried in the Balgay. Cremation had never entered my head. It was rare among working-class folk in 1949. Then I remembered the letter from a *Courier* reader which named the Lochee church where Bob Crumley had married his Jessie, and which stressed her long association with the church. If there was a stone, perhaps there . . . ?

The road to Lochee passed a sign to the crematorium. I turned off on the impulse which led me to the knowledge I did not want to know. He had been cremated. There was no stone. The ashes had been scattered in the crematorium garden.

The woman who imparted this information was a saint. Her manner was courteous and demonstrated unambiguously that she cared how the information would affect me. She brought the book, yet another huge tome of names, to the counter and read out the entry:

'Robert Walker Crumley, 4 Benvie Road, died January 27th 1949, cremated on the 29th.'

It was the kindness of that woman's demeanour more than any

other single emotion which I took out into the crematorium garden. I had never walked in a crematorium garden before, never realised that it would be full of substitute graves – trees, plants, flimsy plaques, benches. If there is a single moment in my life I would not wish on my worst enemy it is that one; that deluge of incomprehensible loneliness, that stupefying helplessness. I remember the press of strewn acorns through the soles of my shoes, the discreet shuttling of black limousines, the indiscreet belching of oblivious traffic outside, where the living city got on with the business of being a living city. I sat on a bench which gave thanks for the life of someone called Edith. I thought: 'How strange, to remember someone with a gift to bring comfort to the tired arses of others,' and I laughed aloud at myself and then couldn't think of a single thing to do, nor a single place to go.

I pulled the death certificate out of my pocket. I read:

'Robert Walker Crumley. Messenger (Corporation) (Retired). Married to 1st Jean Anderson [it says Jane on her gravestone] 2nd Jessie Hill or Strachan . . . ' He had been 72, so was probably born in 1876.

So 120 years later you buy a piece of paper which tells you only that he had been a Corporation messenger.

It is not enough.

Yet who could know that forty-six years after his death. I would come curiously to seek out the grandfather who died when he was eighteen months old, the grandfather who had been denied to him because his forebears saw fit to do so?

Somehow I had imagined that when it came to an interview with an official there would be a tapping of computer keys and a flicker of a name on a screen. It was some comfort, now that I think about it, to find my grandfather in a great book. His death comes alive out of that page, like finding pressed flowers. There is no life left but what you find is the confirmation that a life was lived, commemorated in copperplate fountain pen, the confident handwriting and musty fluency of a certain age, an age of ration books and trams and leeries kindling the pale haloes of gas street-lights, and the brave new post-war world and its cautious hopes. It is an age on the very edge of my memory, and there is another scrap of comfort in the new knowledge that Bob Crumley and I shared it for eighteen months, even though he was failing and blind and I was a lusty nappy-filler. If I heard it once from my mother, I heard it a hundred times, the words with which the midwife greeted my father when I was born:

'You've got a football player there, Mr Crumley,' and though he is reputed to have laughed gleefully, I wonder if a darker shadow crossed his mind even at that moment, at the sound of the words.

Benvie Road is a long steep street unrelieved by gardens. It is, like so many turn-of-the-century Dundee backstreets, walled in by tenements, and . . . well . . . drab. Only in the top corner of the street has the mud-coloured stone been replaced by new brick-built homes. Whether or not you like the dour character of such streets, the brick houses are foreign to it, not belonging. Number four Benvie Road was one of the closes which were demolished to make way for the bricks. No matter. There is enough to give me a feel of the street my grandfather was accustomed to step into the last few years of his life. And I remembered enough of that stony era to put back the gas lamps, the cobbles, the reek in the lums, the working horses and the small black saloon cars with running-boards, not that streets like this would boast many cars then. But in my mind's eye that October day, I had the gist of it. I know now that my grandfather's was a ground-floor flat, and all down the street are ground-floor windows with sills low enough to sit on with your feet comfortably on the pavement.

Peter Cavanagh, who had been the first to contact the *Courier* in response to the article about Bob Crumley, had lived at No. 1b as a child, directly opposite his house. I phoned him.

'I'm talking about the years 1941–43. He often sat on the windowsill when we played football in the street. He was quite tall and thin and bent, an old man, and he wore a bunnet. And he was blind.'

Yes, I thought, and knowing his ability to read a game aloud for the benefit of his fellow sufferers, he was probably following in his head every move the street football bairns made.

'We knew he was the goalie in the cup-winning team, but we never spoke to him and he never spoke to us. Mind you, we didn't go up to him and say "Hiya, Mr Crumley, weren't you the famous goalie?". Bairns had a more respectful attitude to adults then.'

'Unapproachable' was the word he had used in the *Courier*.

But then there was a call to the paper from Ian Roxburgh, whose grandfather had lived upstairs from mine, and who visited him for Saturday lunch. I phoned him, too.

'He was a really friendly man. I always spoke to him when I met him. My grandfather told me all about him, and he would chat away. He was tall and walked with a white stick. He would walk all the way down Benvie Road to a corner shop at the bottom for his milk, tapping his stick all the way. He wasn't stooped, mind. He was as straight as a die.

'When he died there was a big turn-out at the funeral. A lot of the Dundee players were there and the manager – I suppose that would be George Anderson then.'

George Anderson it was, and a few months later he would sign a tall, thin, seventeen-year-old goalkeeper called Bill Brown, and when, five years after that, Alfie took me to Dens for the first time he pointed out Buhll Broon and said:

'There . . . the best goalie Dundee's had since your granfaither.'

So from what I knew and from what I have learned, the milestones of Bob Crumley's life are more or less in place. I have been able to sketch in a handful of details, but the deeper mysteries remain to be the subject of my best guesses. There is no one alive now who can help me and they are the kind of mysteries which are not written down. And I have tangible links: three photographs of the footballer, Dens Park on a Saturday afternoon, Benvie Road without the windowsill, the testimony of an uncle I didn't know I had, the volunteered details from kind strangers.

I remembered a detail of my conversation with Doug Crumley. He described 'Uncle Bob's' earlier house in Lochee High Street, how it caught his imagination because you went into the close off the High Street, then through the back into a garden, and there was another house behind the High Street tenements and shops. Lochee has been crudely remodelled in the intervening seventy-odd years, but I was passing the close mouth anyway on another mission, and I turned in, knowing full well that there is hardly a single old building standing anywhere behind the frontage of the High Street. Through the close, the ground opened out, the traffic noise all but vanished, the souvenirs of many demolitions were all around. I stood there blinking. The one building unblemished by Lochee's endless upheavals was the one Doug had described. A self-contained block of flats three storeys high, directly behind the close and its long garden, and carefully renovated . . . for a moment I was so surprised at its survival that I half-expected the clatter of studs on the stair and the emergence of a lanky young man bouncing a ball. But I'm *that* not good at summoning ghosts. I still wish there had been a gravestone.

Chapter Ten

The Hahky, the Blahcky, and the Lower Pleasance

If you trod the road and the miles to Dundee from the west two or three hundred years ago, along the Tay from Perth, your last eastward mile before the grey throng of the city streets beyond the West Port would have followed a quiet hill track which rose gently above the river's boggy shore. From the top of that hill, all the city and all its river spectacle were laid bare. It would be a fair place on a good day, the top of the Hawk Hill.

In time, the hill grew a tight little village and, in the manner of industrial muscle-flexing cities, in time Dundee swallowed it whole, the way it has swallowed a clutch of villages in its mud-brown maw; a beached whale on its riverbank with a bellyful of Jonahs.

The Hawkhill, in its urbanised prime, was narrowed canyonesque and as raucous as a gannetry in June and probably reeked just as appetisingly, too. And, given that it was a sliver of Dundee, it became the Hahky, at least it did to everyone apart from the mannie who put up the street signs. For long enough, it worked well enough. It was its own place, and it serviced itself with shops and tradesmen and schools and kirks and pubs (fourteen of these, drouthy place that it must have been), and if you were born to it there was little enough reason for you to think of leaving it, or 'going into town' for that matter. What did 'Town' have that you didn't have on your doorstep? You wore your Hahky status like a badge and Dundee was the wolf at the door. Then the wolf became the whale and swallowed you whole, and they built the Perthy and began to stitch fashionable suburbs beyond your suddenly unfashionable little realm and a species of rot set in. And (looking at it now – Eh wisnae there at the time) it seems that where the Hahky met the new po-faced Perthy at the Sinderins, the Victorian preoccupation with veneer at all costs grafted on two hundred yards of posh tenements so that the coarse reality of life within the canyon would not intrude on the airy places beyond where they strutted their stuff. I never did see eye to eye with the Victorians.

Aye, but there's the rub. All that's demonstrably left of the canyon is the posh Victorian bit. It calls itself Gowrie Place, and the flats have stone pillars and iron railings and decorated ground-floor lintels, and the carved date 1863, and that's it. Some of the Jonahs which Dundee swallowed have survived tolerably well: there's as much vigour in Lochee as ever, for example. But the Hahky has suc-cumbed to the incarceration, and the road which now bears the name of Hawkhill is nothing of the kind. You can, of course, get too pre-cious and sentimental about demolished tenements. There is plenty of living testimony to the squalor of the lowest ebb of the Hahky's fortunes, which was what was finally demolished in the 1960s, but if you demolish such a purposeful place, banish its population to edge-of-city suburbs which are the antithesis of the community they inhabited, and if you supplant the purposefulness of community with the purposelessness of a car-carrying trough, what have you achieved beyond the unstitching and the fraying of Dundee's social fabric?

A bit strong? Then walk this way, and remember as you walk the hill of hawks, the country road above the river, and the vigorous ten-emented village which were the natural succession until the Hawkhill was turned over to . . . well, to this.

Let's begin with the posh part, or as posh as it gets, at the west end, opposite McCheyne Church. Feast on that treasury of well-worked and well-cherished stone, handsomely proportioned and wondrously spired. It is all the architecture worth the name you will see for some time. Deep breath, left turn, up the Hahky with you! Gowrie Place of the pillars and railings are sound tenements, but in two hundred yards it disintegrates, and you wince at the sight of the venerable Hawkhill Tavern flanked by pink breeze-block plug-the-gap flats quite unworthy of the stone ring which is implied by the word 'tenement'. There is stone of a kind in the Hawkhill Medical Centre, but only on its outer wall and in the thoughtless gesture of a patch of stone facing. Here is carelessness and blandness and no shred of thought given to what was here or what ought to be here. The other side of the road has fared no better. It too has been demolished and replaced with carparks and patches of landscaped grass with stubborn shrubs, a tradesman's entrance into the now prosperous little enclave of the Perthy. It takes a lot of pride-swallowing for old Hahky natives to see their inheritance usurped so that a quite separate neighbouring community can be better served.

But walk on. Here is Hawkhill Court, which is the kind of not-what-it-seems name we bestow on a small industrial estate these days. You cast your eye round its repertoire of flimsy prefabrications, and you scan the list of their occupants, a list with names like 'Finesse Superslice' and you wonder how we managed to travel so far away from a sense of place in such a short time. It is a superslice of nae finesse whatsoever which has been cut into the map of Dundee where the Hahky once rose and fell on its low hill.

Here is an extinct church at the foot of Ure Street, which looks like a lost Free Church cube from some outpost of Skye, the diametrically opposed definition of God from the one which spired McCheyne Church so gracefully. But God has flitted from here now that two or three no longer gather in his name. There is no particular shame in a redundant church, of course, and many a kirk has found a new lease of life after having been deprived for whatever reason of its congregation. This one, though, has fared less well. It was never a graceful building, and I suspect, belonged to that species of Christianity which glorified simplicity and absence of ornament. Well, it boasts a degree of plainness now which even its most passionate zealots would have decried. Bricks for windows, and one window has even had a hoist slung from it. Whatever it was that required to be hoisted in and out of its old sanctity, it was not souls to be saved. I feel sad, inexplicably sad, at its forlornness. Architecturally, it's worth no more than the health centre, a graceless shell, and probably no more graced when it was more than a shell. But I know a hundred churches like this, for I am an itinerant islander by inclination forbye a mainlander by birth. And while I am no lingerer inside church walls (although St Paul's in the Nethergate once cringed at my youthful tenor) I have stood on Skye headlands and been moved beyond words or reason by the wind that carried Gaelic psalms to my ears from churches like these. I have no way of knowing whether this church-turned-industrial-estate ever heard a Gaelic psalm – probably not, this being the Hahky rather than Tarskavaig – but its dead-on-it's feet survival is one more unworthiness in the street.

'Look, Jimmy, if God was that worried,' Alfie'd say, 'he'd miracle the hale jingbang awa tull yur Tarrywhu'si 'snem, rebuhld it stane beh stane and fuhll it wi psalmsters, an ah the locals on Skeh'd take ain look it an say "Whar the hell did God find a kirk wi such ugly muddybroon wahs as that?"'

I was about to offer protest. Alfie, realistic to a fault, breenged on:

'Yur an ehdealist, Jimmy, an Dundee's no a place fur ehdealists. Huv ye no learned yet that Dundonians is the only fowk on the planet that acshully likes wur stane this colour? Ahbdy else on the planet'd throw a street party the day they cah'd a this shite doon. Eh'm no sayin they've improved things, bu whu they cah'd doon was shite, Jimmy, an that goes fur yer kirk an ah.'

So I stand outside my dead-on-its-feet kirk and cast an eye on the huge gap which is its neighbour, and I peer for the moment into a great wound in the side of my city, the bones showing through in the half-demolished roofs and walls of yesterday's industrial endeavours. New development has begun. There is a pattern of streets on the ground, lamp standards in position, and the first bricks are laid. They form a zig-zag of low wall, presumably carparking spaces, and one hundred yards of brick pavement under the west wall of the church. The bricks are pink.

Demolition has let the sky in here, and opened wide views where there were canyon walls. Some of them are worth looking at, too, like the surprise of the Lah Hull where the Hahky collides with the Blahcky. The Lah is to Dundee what the Cuillin are to Skye, forever cropping up when you expect to see something else, and from the unlikeliest of places. Other views, like the platoon of multis plouter-ing down the city skyline, were better screened by the canyon walls. It's funny how you crave canyon walls when there's nothing higher at the roadside than the pavement.

The university is the biggest imprint on the Hawkhill now, the kind of concrete monolith which the 1960s thought was a good idea. It turns its back on the street, shades some of its bulk with trees and grass banks, but doesn't disguise the fact that it's the service entrance which the Hawk hill attends to. 'Street' is the wrong word here, because there is no sense of street, only road, only the swift passage of traffic cutting through urban aimlessness. Any unknowing eye would find little enough wrong. Those of us who call cities home all have concrete crosses to bear, and many a concrete cross is far more sparing with the greenery than the University campus.

So what's the problem? I stand on the highest curve of pavement on a quiet Saturday morning, the sun half roused and sluggish, and balancing out in my mind what I once heard a Dundee councillor describe as 'the pros and cons for and the pros and cons against'. An old streetwise and self-contained place, admittedly turned squalid and not half the place it once was, and sluggish as that sun, was demol-ished. In its place, and reflecting the city's changing priorities, is space, a wide traffic-friendly-but-going-nowhere-in-particular road, and the turned backs of the Perthy and the University. There is a gnawing unease, this somnolent Saturday. I try to pluck it from the recesses of the mind and hang it on the wind in front of me so that I can scrutinise it, but all I get back is a verdict on the University: why are centres of education and enlightenment always so plug-ugly? It isn't helpful. What I want is for a real human voice, the one which took the final decision for this re-working of quintessential Dundee into quisling new-town anywhere, to answer in words I can under-stand my single question: why?

No, it's not a single question. It's:

(a) Why have you done this to my city?
(b) Why is this better than restoring or rebuilding what was?
(c) Why in this most distinctive and harmonious of cities have you settled for every other city's discordance?

(d) Why, given that all cities must evolve, must you evolve away the quintessential?

But the questions grow too complex for this monumental simplicity. The Hawkhill was not just demolished. It was removed. It was super-sliced into oblivion. No attempt was made to honour its existence, and don't insult us by pointing to the streetnames on the signposts. We, the body of the city, have lost a limb, and we feel the pain of the wound, that wound in the limb which isn't there. That gnawing unease is the pain.

It is an irresistible and endlessly resurfacing theme in any consideration of Dundee's townscape, because it challenges the present and the future with the most powerful force known to mankind – our love and longing for our own past. In Dundee of all places, we consummate that love with rare passion. Why else relay tramlines in the Murraygate with no prospect of trams; why bring back the *Discovery*; why the Verdant Mill; why the bookshop obsession with all-our-yesterdays photographs to be pored over through mud-tinted glasses? Some of it is our very recent past, too, and the obsession dates from the point at which we stopped building wi wur ain stane. The old Hahky, whatever its deathbed faults, was built wi wur ain stane. So was that sad kirk, and whatever they build next door, if it's in pink brick, it won't be finding its way to anyone's bookshelf, or into anyone's heart. It is an unarguable truth that one of the reasons why we have so acclaimed the pedestrianising of a large area of downtown Dundee, and one of the reasons why we now keep it so much cleaner than it used to be, is because the project has ripped up tarmac and given us back stone setts. For tarmac read pink brick. It's the same argument.

Streets like the Hahky were the Dundee we care about. What has replaced the Hahky is the Dundee we couldn't care less about. We have lost the mud-coloured stone and the setts and we have got tarmac and pink brick and we think it stinks. Alfie, now that he's clocked up thirty years in his between-the-wars council house on the side of the Lah, taps me on the shoulder and points to that sentence in Chapter Six about my grandfather's house in Logie Street.

'Eh quote, Jimmy,' I hear him say, 'your very words':

"' . . . the house long demolished and a good thing too . . .'"

I did say that, didn't I? I had the smell of the place and the dying breath of my grandmother and the grotesque mousetrap in my head when I wrote it.

'The Hakhy they cah'd doon was a mile o smelly hooses an dyin breaths and moosetraps, and bairns dyin in their beds 'n' ah forbye the ahld folk. That's what the Hahky'd turned intil, Jimmy. It wiz festerin.

'So ye see, Jimmy, yer wrang, an yer right as well. Ye were willin tae cah doon yer granfaither's hoose because you kenned ah aboo whu went on there. But naebdy else's hooses uv tae go, eh? Tha' cannae be right. Bu' it wuz the basis, or at least the excuse they offered, for cahin doon when they could uv restored, or carefully rebuilt. Uv coorse demolition wiz ah the rage in this toon in they days, an you an me ken how tha wiz, an so diz ahbdy else in this toon. Bu it wiznae a good enough excuse. So yer right to say that they shouldnae be cah'd doon. Ken whu they should uv done up the Hahky. A fehr! Burnt the insides o the hooses oot, then put them back, new roofs 'n' ah.'

'Eh've never heard o fehr as a tool o urban regeneration, Alfie,' says Eh.

'Ken how yur ayeways on aboo yur pine wuds up in the Cairngorms? Ken how ye tellt iz that ane o the best weys o regeneratin the wuds is a fehr . . . creates a good seedbed? Well, it's the same thing. Burn oot the crap and lay the seedbed o a new generation o hooses. The wahs, the mud-broon stane yer aye on aboo . . . tha's yur granny pines that chuck the seed owre ah the pliss. Save the pine wuds. Save wur mud-broon wahs. It's the same thing, Jimmy. Yer aye on aboo' a sense o pliss. It's the same bloody thing.'

The fire has got to Blackness Hall, and some time ago by the look of it. I have just caught sight of it, standing in a dwam at the West Port end of the Hawkhill where it headbutts into Blackness Road's midriff. Something stirs, subduing the unease; a kindlier something. Throughout the 1960s, drunk on the Shadows, I brandished a succession of cheap guitars and towed a ghastly black amplifier and Watkins Copycat echo unit in and out of the ranks of a series of what we were pleased to call beat groups. I never wanted to sing, only to play the Hank Marvin bits. Some of the groups even worked, a couple were paid for the working. Rehearsal spaces were everywhere in demolition-happy Dundee. The most bizarre was a spiritualist church in the Wellgate, where the, er . . . preacher tried to convince me I could be a good medium. I don't want to be medium I told him. I want to be brilliant. I think he didn't laugh.

But there would come a time when I went legit. I joined a dance band. If memory serves correctly, and there is no reason why it should, given the number of bad gigs in bad venues I played that heady decade (and you know what they say about the '60s – if you were there you can't remember if you can remember, you weren't there) . . . if memory serves, my first dance band gig was a wedding reception in the Blackness Hall. My guitar was new. No it wasn't, it was ancient but it was new to me, it cost £30, it looked more like Bert Weedon's than Hank Marvin's, and I bought it in the West Port, in a shop called Musical Supplies. It was probably the worst guitar Hofner ever built, a white semi-acoustic with bolt-on electrics. The electrics would prove its downfall on its stage debut.

The single pick-up was part of a chrome scratchboard, the jack plug was tiny, and the lead uniquely flimsy, and short. Spare leads were simply not to be had. I think extension leads for amplifiers had not yet been invented, or if they had, they were quite outwith my sphere. Electrically, I was an ignoramus, a quality, I shared, apparently, with whoever had wired Blackness Hall, for the only socket at my disposal was halfway up the wall. I looked at the yardage available from my leads, I looked at the gap between the edge of the stage and the wall, and I had problems. The seen-it-all-before accordionist devised a solution. Amplifier on chair against wall, guitarist on very edge of stage. Lead trails down, across passage and up to amplifier. Neither of us could know, could we, that the passage was the only access to the ladies loo. Neither of us could have foreseen, could we, that the first person to require access was the bride.

We had negotiated the bridal waltz ('Edelweiss', 'Moon River', 'The Anniversary Waltz') and were just getting into our full-blown, all-stomping, three-piece stride with the first foxtrot ('The Lady is A Tramp', 'Bill Bailey', 'Whispering') when the bride suddenly discarded her dancing partner, turned for the loo passage, and ran. 'Ran' does not quite catch the gist of her progress, but she was fast for someone in four-inch heels, two feet of beehived hair and a furlong of flowing train over one arm, mostly. The wind resistance must have been formidable. She reached me, her heel snagged on the guitar lead, the very stiff plug at the guitar end resisted the tug. She fell full length. She severed the lead at the jack plug. She picked herself up still clutching the train and, without a word, she vanished into the toilet. I looked around the hall. Not a soul had noticed. I looked at the accordionist who shrugged, not an easy thing to do when you are wearing an accordion. He said later that he'd thought he heard something off the beat. I mimed through the second half of 'Bill Hailey' and all of 'Whispering'.

The toilet door creaked behind me. I half turned, fearful of bridal retribution, but she emerged beaming wondrously at me, unscathed beyond a degree of dishevelment in the beehive. She put a hand on my shoulder, planted a kiss on my cheek reeking sensationally to my eighteen-year-old sensibilities of what I now know to be gin and thick perfume and whispered tantalisingly close to my ear:

'That was the happiest piss of my life.'

Then she sashayed out into the middle of the floor, grabbed a passing man, threw both arms round his neck, laid her head on his startled shoulder from which position she winked at me and said (I presume it was a musical request):

'Smooch, guitar man, smooch.'

So I mimed while the accordion played 'Stranger On The Shore'. Ah, the sixties, how they swung.

I wish the Blackness Hall a healthy restoration, and sooner rather than later, a prosperous regeneration out of the seedbed of its fire. Its survival is tenuous as long as it remains a mud-coloured shell, over-cooked round the edges. We are not so well served with free-standing old stone survivors in this part of town that we can discard another one.

The Blahcky Ha' is not alone. Its near-neighbour on the Larch Street–Daniel Street corner is boarded up and cobwebbed with that gossamer shroud of over-long vacancy. Here is a building to put the superslicers and anonymous architectural fly-by-nighters to shame; it is unsung in the roll-call of the great monolithic muhlls, appears in no exploration of Dundee's architecture, but among what remains of the Blahcky, and the Hahky, it is a thing to stumble across and wonder at for its style, for its architectural class. I confess its presence took me by surprise, its handsome little courtyard entrance more like the front elevation of a Royal Mile mansion in Edinburgh than a forgotten Dundee factory, for of that triumvirate of streets which bears down on the city centre from the west, only the Blahcky is remotely recognisable for what it was. The Hahky, as we have seen, is a sham, and that much-built-upon valley to the north of the Blahcky where once the Scouringburn ran to the bleachers at Meadowside, now flows bleakly through an ad-hocery of no-man's-lands where planning has been at best casual, at worst absent.

It is more trough than valley. You half expect troglodytes to emerge from its pends and closes. Every city has these pockets. The thrust of renewal and civic initiative is forever elsewhere, and you wonder how things came to such a pass. So you scratch at the surface of so-familiar streets, a handful of plasterwork crumbles and spills a few beans and has-beens and, in such company, the unsung courtyard of Daniel Street is an anthem.

There are those, of course, who will tell you that a great service was performed by the demolitioners hereabouts, and spit the words 'Blue Mountains' at you by way of all-purpose justification. The Blue Mountains had a legendary notoriety. 'Ye dinnae wahn' tae go in there son, they eat thur young up the Blue Mountains.' Childhood memory coughs up the shadow of them rather than the substance, a huddle of high, fog-bound tenements that walled-in perpetually dark and dire streets, something like that. The impression given by some of Dundee's louder reforming demolitionists is that the very concept of urban deprivation was born there. I simply don't remember them, but I remember the threat the words carried. Alfie's Ma, though, she remembered.

'Social deprivation meh fu'!' she rebuked me. She's ninety and fit as Jimmy Shand's fiddle as she reminded me, and whether it had slipped her mind that Jimmy plays the accordion, or whether she was making merry at my expense, I was never sure. Anyway, 'slum' was a four-letter word she didn't much care for.

'We looked after wur ain. Ahbdy looked efter ahbdy else. We didnae need social workers an tha' kind o fancy stuff. Folk's owre saft. Whu's a-dae wi them ah? Whu's wrang wi workin folk bidin in workin hooses? Keep yer mansions an yer semis. We wur fehv bairns an wur parents, an ah kinds o ithers fae time to time. Ahbdy wiz aye drappin in. Ah tha' in twa rooms an a scullery.

'Rats? Uv coorse thur wiz rats. So whu? Us bairns used to chase them in the cellars. See, thur wiz a trapdoor in the closies, an steps led doon intul the cellars. The cellars run ah the weh underneath the hooses, like the length o fower closies. An tha's whar we chased the rats. We got a belt in the lug if we go fund oo, but we were aye ge'in belts in the lug. It wiz ain o the things as happened tull ye when ye were a bairn. You go' skelpt. Eh wiz wahtchin the telly, ken, the Question Time' stuff wi the laddie Dimbleby, and some hoity-toity wifie wiz blahin awa aboo' no lettin wiz spank wur bairns. "Spank!" Tha wiz the wurd she kep usin. "Spank!" Eh laughed mesel sully. Eh never got spanked in meh life. Eh go' belti', Eh go' skelpt, Eh go' thumpt, Eh go' cuffed in the lug. An ah tha time, Eh niver once fel Eh wisnae loved. Love, son. Tha's whu' works. No the European Coor o Human Bloody Rights. Love. That's a human right, the only ane as ma'ers. Ye cannae ge' tha' fae a court in Europe or any ither pliss.

'Eh, we had rats. Bu we had love, an it wisnae jist wir ain hoose, it wiz aroon us, an that's no jist the haverins o an ahld wifie wi her rose-tinti't specs on, son, that's the truth.

'Oh eh! Eh wiz tellin you aboo' the rats.

'Well, ae day, we chased them right alang the cellars an we decided to go up intul the last closie and wahk back alang the street, rather than wahk back through the cellars tul wur ain closie. Well, ane o the laddies goes up the steps an gies the trap door a shove. Wouldnae budge. Anither laddie trehs. Wouldnae budge. The baith oh them trehs. Wouldnae budge. Now we could just uv wahked back through the cellars bu' this wiz a new gemme an we didnae hae tha' mony new gemmes, so we jist ba'ered awa at the trapdoor.

'Suddenly, thur wiz this affy rippin noise and a thump, an the door wen' fleein up, an we were in an ahld wifie's livin-room! There wiz fowre o them, ahld wifies, sittin roond lookin at us, an the first one picked up a stick and gied the laddy such a thump on es heid . . .'

And at that, the tears of mirth rolled down Alfie's Ma's cheeks, and her shoulders heaved, and for five minutes you couldn't get a word of sense out of the three of us, and we laughed until it hurt.

'We jist aye thought tha' ah the trapdoors wen' intae closies. We'd gone right through the ahld wifie's lino!'

And she was away again, and the shadows that had lain for so long in my mind at the sound of the words 'Blue Mountains' were blown away forever, and in the place of their many infamies I have a picture of an old wifie in her wee sheltered house in the Ferry (which she likes well enough . . . 'it's grand . . . at meh age') with the tears rolling down her face, and that face creased and flushed with the helplessness of her laughter, and replete with that sense of love which you cannot buy in a court and which had served her all her days and outfaced the social deprivation of the Blue Mountains.

There are other infamies, other shadows thrown, hereabouts.

Other walls rise, almost as mountainous, not blue, but a troubling mud-brown cliff erect among the city's undulating contours, a pared-to-the-bone survivor from that earliest nineteenth-century jute mill era when the barons battled for the best sites on the banks of the Scouringburn. It is that sinister bulk which thrusts itself darkly up out of the city heat haze from the Tap o the Lah, the one with the stubby square tower for a front door geegaw, the one where the ghost of a mill lass with long hair screams at tail-between-the-legs cats and the unseen sky-yapping of homing geese on star-black winter nights. The Coffin Mill.

Remembering the teenage knee-trembling it induced when I cycled past it and realising it had not darkened my passing for perhaps twenty years, and having now decided to meet the thing head-on, alone and on foot (why? The writer making demands on the body it inhabits, that's why!), I took a blazing hot mid-afternoon to it, tempting as little fate as possible, everything hard-edged and logical, no half-light where half-truths might swither. The first sight of it from pavement level unlocked the specific source of the cyclist-fear, freed it from its long captivity in an unsuspected reservoir of memory. My brother, Vic, used to do a Saturday morning butcher round hereabouts. (I was usually too involved in football or cricket for such fund-raising enterprise.) One Saturday he was ill and I deputised at short notice, uncertain of the shop's location, uncertain of the round, unenthused even by the prospect of nicking 7/6d (or whatever) from his amassing fortune. I was still unreassured when I left the butcher's shop. The proprietor was a butcher, not a social worker. He saw no reason to be grateful. He was paying me, after all. I left the shop hesitantly, and rode straight into the winter shadow of the Coffin Mill, whose story I knew, but whose cathedral bulk I had probably not encountered in the raw before. Its black depths hurled a bellowing black dog at my wheels. I have had dogs jump at my bike before, but the combination of the dog's gloomy provenance and the fact that I had a saddlebag full of sausages, mince, and chops leaking blood into brown paper wrappings accounted for the unnerving nature of the moment. I lost my nerve, lost control of the bike and hit the cobbles as the dog advanced.

Enter St Christopher, the traveller's saint, or if not he, then whoever predetermined that morning's distribution of D.P.M. milk floats. The restless percussiveness of milk bottles on the move down a cobbled street took the dog's eye off the main chance, the float hurtled downhill between the dog and my predicament, and by the time it had passed I was remounted and mobile, and the blackened windows of the Coffin Mill blurred past.

Now, perhaps thirty-five years after the event, that dog suddenly rematerialised in my mind with all the black drama of nightmare, and I felt again my legs flaying at disobedient pedals, saw the road tilt to meet my fall. I felt cold in that heatwave's uncompromising blast.

The Coffin Mill is a castle with a stone moat, a grim industrial citadel. I think I loathe it more vehemently than any other pile of built stone that ever threw a shadow, for indefinable reasons that have nothing whatever to do with the dog.

Its stone felt warm to the touch. Why wouldn't it in the third unbroken week of an August heatwave? I walked into the stone moat from the main road, that cart-wide alley which laps two sides of the mill, narrowly detaching it from the rest of the world, and named with Dundee's characteristically and sometimes fiendishly black humour 'The Lower Pleasance'. The name is older than the mill, of course, but it is an ill-at-ease juxtaposition, the coffin of cathedral dimensions and the devilish smirk of some nineteenth-century sign-writer as he nailed his signs to the brutish walls. Scottish castles – real ones, not jute ones – often had a park attached, the Pleasance, and it does not take a great leap of the imagination to suppose that the first Lower Pleasance was the lowest-lying acreage of Dudhope Castle's parks while Dundee was still far off, and huddled close to its shore.

Ah, but that was then. The great muhll has risen and the city has swarmed round it like an invading army, but like many a great castle in its heyday, it has proved all but impregnable, its dark forces repelling all attempts at civilising its dark occupancy. I was faintly appalled to discover that a start had been made at converting the Coffin Mill into housing. It has been done successfully often enough elsewhere, but here even that benevolent intention has foundered. The new windows have been smashed, new concrete staircases mount the void. The goon box-tower was to have been someone's high-and slate-canopied home of distinction, draped in estate-agency clichés. And haunted. You would be able to look down on the vast coffin-shaped monstrosity from there, master of all the ill-starred ambience you survey.

But whatever the reason, whatever the negative nature of the conspiracy levelled at the venture, it has failed. The Lower Pleasance offers the ghoul-curious a glimpse within. The padlocked and barbed-wire gates hold nothing back. You peer through at the court-yard in its high summer dark shadow, peer at the abandoned debris of renovation, peer at the black-windowed cell-blockishness of the walls, and you feel oppression come at you in waves. You wonder who on earth dreamed an architect's dreams in the midst of such tangible malevolence. The eye-wincing sunlight of the day, so benevolent on other walls, only throws blacker, harder-edged shadows into the gaunt gate of the Coffin Mill.

I harbour this ambition for the Coffin Mill, I who so heartily champion the cause of the mud-coloured stone in all its built forms other than this one and my Grampa's house – it is that the thing should be swept from the landscape of Dundee without trace, and in its place there should be a garden, a place of light and space and an absence of walls, an enlightening oasis to gladden the heart of that triumvirate of streets, the Hahky, the Blahcky and the Lower Pleasance. Having demolished the fearful ahld muhll, we can ship its old stone bones to some repository of mud-coloured building materials to be used either to patch gaps in threadbare streets or to see if we can still build new houses with the stuff. There is a wheen of houses lying unbuilt in that treasury of Dundee stone which is the walls and tower of the Coffin Mill, and enough slate to roof them all. Now there is a vision worth dreaming for an architect: new Dundee houses without a pink brick in sight.

So I walked the entire length of the back and north flank of the mill, which is all the Lower Pleasance there is, a dispiriting roofless tunnel of a thing, and tried to fill my mind with imagery of patient carthorses and singing jute lassies and barefoot bairns and all the caterwauling stushie of the mill, the full-throated roar of its industrial might. It must have been some bellow. It must have sucked the houses dry for a mile around in every direction, sucked every close-mouth dry of its women and men folk and bent their backs and dinned their lugs with its tyranny. In every house, every long toilsome day, there were empty rooms, or ahld folk, or bairns, or a few disgruntled men (for the jute mills were thirstier for woman workers than men), an eerily lop-sided society every working day. Imagine the lane at lousin time, thick with that grimy, liberated army. At that moment alone, of every working day, there might have been pleasance here.

Sunlight floods in at the far end of the Lower Pleasance, where it reaches the head of the coffin in Brewery Lane (no brewery, of course, any more than there is pleasance in the Lower Pleasance). You step into the heat, into the life of the sunlight after the sterile shadows, and you raise your eyes and there is the Lah Hull corn-gold, sunlit friend, the Upper Pleasance. There is Alfie at your side, having declined your invitation to circumnavigate the brute. He fixes an eye on the sun-worshipper, squints back down the length of the lane, and demands:

'Satisfehd?'

You nod. He shrugs, aghast at your folly.

'An whu in the name o the wee man wiz tha' ah aboo'?'

'Search me, Alfie.'

Chapter Eleven

Not Glorious, Yet Not Contemptible

Time present and time past
Are both perhaps present in time future,
And time future contained in time past.
— FOUR QUARTETS, T.S. Eliot

What's this? T.S. Eliot! Hardly Dundee's kind of poet, eh? We who are perpetually saddled with the legacy of McGonagall? Not that that's the burden some outsiders seem to think. Dundee has always had a soft spot for nutters, always offered them asylum, as Alfie would say. But Eliot? We would seem to have no more use for the rarified vocabulary of his *Four Quartets* ('inoperancy', 'appetency', 'eructation') than he would appear to have for ours ('bacherties', 'cundie', 'ple'ie'), we who wear our intellectualism lightly smokescreened by dafties and Desperate Dans.

Now and then, though, the mask slips to reveal a poet, a painter, a singer, a playwright, and unaccustomed colour plays among the mud-coloured walls. Dundee's great theme is itself, and here am I, caught in the act of heaping more coals on that fire. And when Dundee considers itself, it almost always considers itself as a poor echo of its past.

127

'Wur a toon full o time traivellers, Jimmy,' Alfie'd say, 'an the only journey we ken is bacherties.'

So I quoted Eliot at him, as above, and added, 'The Dundee condition. We should have put a statue to Eliot in the Albert Square aside Burns.'

'Fine beh me, though uv coorse Burns said it be'er . . . but then Burns said ahthin be'er nor ahb'dy. Mind "Tae a Moose"?'

'To a Mouse, Alfie. He didnae . . . '

'Whu ur ye on aboo?'

'He called it To a Mouse.'

'Eh, Tae a Moose. That's whu Eh jist said.'

'Right. Carry on.'

'Still thou art blesst compared wi me,

The present only touches thee

But aft Eh bacherties cast meh ee

On prospects drear

An forrit, though Eh canna see

Eh guess an fear . . . 'S that no beautiful or whu'?'

'S.F.P., Alfie.'

The real grain of truth in the Burns of it is that those backward prospects were so drear, at least they were when they were the present, when this present now was their future, still guessed and feared at. But how we all leap — and with what passion! — to the defence and the deification of that Dundee that was, that time past. Compared to that past which had its last confident throw of the dice in the 1950s (my childhood years so I write as one who grew up on its cusp), Dundee's present seems stalled and rudderless.

There is much truth in the 'artist's statement' which accompanies Joseph McKenzie's compelling photographic exhibition, 'Dundee – City in Transition', a collection of over four hundred black-and-white 1960s prints now owned by the McManus Galleries.

'When I came to Dundee to teach photography in 1964 as a complete foreigner-incomer, I was at once pole-axed by the combination of wonderful light and an eroding urban texture of an unsophisticated tradition.

'Slum clearance was activated zealously in the dispersion of the population to green belt suburbs in all the preoccupations about planning, environment and the infrastructure . . . the new in-words.

Cox's Stack – only Dundee has a love affair with a lum

Tay Road Bridge and St Paul's Cathedral spire

The Old Steeple and the Discovery, seen from the Law

Seagoing city – the Tay estuary from the Law

The Old Steeple – four-square landmark and medieval survivor

Made in Scotland from girders – the Tay Bridge

Ancestral home – Bob Crumley's home in Lochee High Street

The Crumley family's second house – and its view – from the Balgay

Eye to the hills – North Dundee and Sidlaws

New Lochee, same old lum

. . . beauty lies in the eye of the gasholder . . .

Lower Pleasance? It's a lie!

The Coffin Mill – 'the thing should be swept from the landscape without trace'

The wondrous old frigate
Unicorn *at her berth*

Curlew on the shore, Broughty Ferry

Stone eagles and mysterious
head, Dock Street

The vision splendid – James Thomson's painting of the re-sited town house

'Much that was the natural inheritance of Dundee like the city centre community of Hawkhill (a potential campus to the university) was swept aside and destroyed in the almost ruthless no-holds-barred opportunism which opened up to those contractors who sensed little sentiment or emotional soul-searching as to the alternative value of preservation of humble abodes. Perhaps Dundee became the most destroyed city on earth?'

McKenzie's work is not just beautifully made. It is also redolent of that emotional soul-searching so lacking in the hewers and fellers of our stone-built heart, our past. The city he found in its pole-axing light was contemplating the abyss. He photographed it as the last rites were being administered and, if you belong to my generation or anything older, you lurch back in McKenzie's provocative prints to that stoorie era of crashing walls, when old stone familiars vaporised before your disbelieving eyes. Each one was a vertebra plucked from the crucial skeleton by which all cities live and breathe. So many were plucked that a species of civic spinelessness was the inevitable consequence. Dundee swung in the '60s alright, on the end of a rope.

But the victim was cut down before it stopped breathing. For the other crucial ingredient in McKenzie's photography is the folk, and while the civic frailties of one administration in particular were as crooked as the Dichty, we – the long-suffering tribe of Dundonians – dug in for one more long siege. Worse villains than Tom Moore have tried to squeeze the breath from our old stone soul in our many turbulent pasts and wur no deid yet. While the stushie and stoor of falling masonry and over-hasty, over-thoughtless redevelopment rang in our ears and rankled our collective thrapple, we drew deep on our inexhaustible well of stoicism; a city of Auntie Megs, and Alfie, as good at Shakespeare as he is at Burns, was forever thrusting Shylock at you, the same two lines:

'Stuhll Eh've bore it wi a patient shrug

Fur sufferance's the badge o ah wur tribe.'

It came as no surprise to find the visitors' book in the McKenzie exhibition bulging with the enthusiasm of thousands of local 'visitors' whose responses to an invitation to comment on the exhibition chorused the same verdict again and again: make it a permanent exhibition. Our preferred direction remains bacherties. Our preferred era is one in which Dundee's beating heart was stone, and those who would now massage the heartbeat back to its fullest vigour must acknowledge that preference, otherwise they cannot take the people of Dundee with them. 'Time future contained in time past . . .'

It has all happened before. Every other page of my venerable *History of Dundee* seems to be studded with paragraphs like this:

In Tucker's Report to the Government of the Lord Protector Cromwell in 1654, one hundred and ninety-two years ago, he speaks of Dundee, its commerce and shipping, thus: The towne of Dundee was sometime a towne of riches and trade, but the many rencontres it hath met with all in the time of domestick commotions, and her obstinacy and pride of late yeares rendering her a prey to the soldier*, have much shaken and abated her grandeur; and notwithstanding all, she remaynes still, though not glorious, yet not contemptible.

*This refers to the capture of the town by Monk, three years before.

Never more eloquently damned with faint praise 'not glorious, yet not contemptible', but not a bad summary of McKenzie's Dundee either, where the obstinacy and pride of the tribe grins robustly out through the 'rencontres' and 'domestick commotions', as it doubtless did when the Victorians inflicted the good intentions of the 1871 Improvement Act on the close-gathered streets of the jute-boom city.

How I loathe the Victorians. How I resent their 'Improvement' zeal. They rubbished our medieval origins and gave us the Royal Arch, a meaningless free-standing facade of unrelieved ugliness, a thunderous waste of good stone quickly blackened by the daily grind of workaholic railway engines which shuttled in and out of the docks under its hideous shadow. The solitary service which the 1960s 'improvements' rendered us was to cart away that monolithic disfigurement. They demolished the High Street's Old Trades Hall and gave us traffic. They flattened the Vault and Castle Court and God knows what else around the old Pillars Town House and established the sad precedent which finally accounted for the Town House itself in 1932, and no amount of public outcry could resist the head of steam generated by Victorian precedent. They swept away Bucklemaker Wynd and left us with Victoria Road, and they made a sycophantic slaverer out of McGonagall:

Let all hatred towards her be thrown aside
All o'er her dominions broad and wide;
And let her subjects bear in mind,
By God kings and queens are put in trust o'er mankind.

Oh, so it's God's fault! But you can never stay mad at McGonagall for long. In the very next verse is his very funniest couplet:

Therefore rejoice and be glad on her Jubilee day,
And try and make the heart of our Queen feel gay;
Oh! try and make her happy in country and town,
And not with Shakespeare say, 'uneasy lies the head that wears a crown'.

The one principle of the Improvement Act which Dundee would have done well to adhere to was that no building should be more than four storeys high. If only . . .

We Dundee folk have all seen our past flattened in the name of someone's definition of improvement, and it would be good to think that at last, now that we know the worth of heritage, now that we practise and preach conservation as a force for good in our midst, we have learned that restoration of that which is well built and characteristic of us can almost always be more fruitful than calling in the demolitioners. It would be nice to think that – wouldn't it?

Alfie shook his head alarmingly one night in The Pillars, that city-centre howff which, like the wee sculptures at Boots Corner, commemorates the past in miniature – a model of the Pillars for a pub sign:

'Yer invitin trouble for yersel wi that line o thought laddie. Somewhere oot there, thurz a laddie the same age as you were when they cahd doon the Overgate, an *his* heritage ull be the mul'is and the Tey Road Bridge, concrete in other words, ah the keech – tae use an architectural phrase – you 'n' Eh cannae abide. Whu' ur you goin tae tell *him* when your Improvement Act of 2000 AD wahnts tae cah doon ahthin owre fower flairs an scrap the road bridge an tak the wa'erfron back intae the realm oh the people?'

Alfie's good at questions. Answers – that's his weakness. But of course, as always, the question of his was a good one.

131

So I thought it out, long and hard, and what I would tell such a laddie is this:

There are two things which hallmark Dundee and set it apart from all other cities, all other places – its situation and its stone. We have the best situation of them all (well . . . maybe Oban has a better one) and the worst stone. But the first principle of thoughtful building in Scotland from the brochs onwards has always been to build with what is to hand. Dundee stands in that tradition. Even the frantic jute-boom building honoured it, and not even the Victorians tried to change the colour of the place, although they tried to change everything else.

Concrete and glass and brick are impostrous to all that, and because they have been universally adopted, they blur our cities' distinctions with a low common denominator which is born of none of them. It does not mean that just because a building is stone it is good and because it is concrete it is bad. There is many a disfiguring pile of stone and Dundee owns a few and there have been demolitions which were thoroughly merited. And there have been beautiful things done in concrete, though not here that I can think of.

But a city evolves in stone, at least old ones do, old ones like Dundee. Our thousand years only contemplated trying to build (arpart from lums) in anything other than our own stone perhaps seventy years ago. So we are a stone-thirled tribe and now that we have lost so much of that to which we are thirled, there should be a presumption against further interference with what remains.

You cannot divide Dundee geographically and historically like Edinburgh into the Old Town and the New Town, a spectacular architectural co-existence. Dundee doesn't go in for architectural co-existence and never has. We had an Ahld Toon. We flattened it. We have a New Toon.

No . . . we didn't flatten it. We had it flattened. But the new town is still punctuated by the old, conscience-prickers in stone, scraps of mud-coloured dignity among the heaped indignities of crass architect-free buildings and planning-free development. In the process of enduring decades of civic thoughtlessness and the odd bout of civic corruption, the built fabric of Dundee has travelled three-quarters of the way towards losing its soul. You cannot redeem that missing 75 per cent, but you must look to what remains and draw inspiration

132

from it, and liberate it from the worst disfigurements of what came after.

For example (I would tell this hypothetical laddie), we have one building in our midst, a lofty and conspicuous miracle (and not the least part of its miracle is its survival) acclaimed by any expert assessment of architecture which ever clapped eyes on it, acclaimed as a wonder, acclaimed for its uniqueness. Here is Ian C. Hannah's characteristically understated assessment of the Old Steeple in his classic work, *The Story of Scotland in Stone:*

The Old Steeple at Dundee is singularly unlike any that could be found in the south. The lowest stage with a very large six-light window (whose principal feature is the common heavy central mullion, branching near the top), ceiled with a lierne vault, was open to the nave by a moulded lancet arch, and corbels indicate the position of a wooden gallery. This portion is supported by heavy buttresses which do not rise above the first stage. The next section is very plain, and the two top storeys with lancet openings are narrower than the rest, allowing a gallery all round. The whole composition is admirably bound together by a stair turret to the top on the northern side. Within the open parapet is a gabled chamber with fire-place, a lofty and exposed dwelling, commanding most extensive Tayside views, This very typically Scottish summit and a rather military character (though without any actual castle features) render this steeple a most effective piece of work, and very individual.

Don't you feel you should applaud?

Shouldn't such matchlessness be venerated, not just in the text books, but on the ground? Especially on the ground? Yet there is not one long or short view of the Old Steeple — not one from any direction — which blots out the tawdry nature of its surroundings. There was a time even in my life (and this is the advantage I have over you, I would tell my reluctant protégé) when what Alfie terms 'the Ahld Steeplie' rose among mud-coloured walls, towering over the Overgate the way York Minster heaves above its crouching townscapes. The Overgate redevelopment was the first of its kind in any Scottish city centre. I venture to say that it is also the worst. It was completed in 1970, and if there is any justice, any civic acknowledgement of the *spirit* of the Old Steeple, the jarring cut-price wretchedness of the invasive Overgate Centre will be gone forever by the turn of the century. It is no way to greet a new millennium to have your solitary fifteenth-century masterpiece stand in the right angle of the two limbs of the worst building in town. Besides, I have a plan.

But before I unbate your breath with that, here is a day in the autumn of 1995, a quiet Saturday 9 a.m. kind of day when the tree-sheen at the Ahld Steeplie's knees and that pole-axeing light as recommended by Jospeh McKenzie caused me to draw my own camera from its scabbard and brandish it meaningfully, before the bemused gaze of a rank-ful of comatose taxi-drivers. Dundee still seems to be taken by surprise that there are people in its midst who now and again behave like tourists, unsheathing cameras, or guidebooks. Tourism is a new phenomenon here, thanks to the *Discovery*, and the fact that someone might pause under the Old Steeple to admire it is still queer. It's just the Old Steeple after all, and it's . . . well, it's ours. Why would someone else want to come and look at it? And because I had a camera in my hand and it was October, not August, I *must* be a tourist and not a wholly sane tourist at that. That was the gist of the taxi-drivers' unspoken speculation.

It had been a handsome early morning on the river, but cloud was thickening over the Bell Rock, thrusting tides of cold air shorewards. I had had the waterfront to myself but now I wanted warmth and coffee and the proximity of the Ahld Steeplie for an hour, and for no good reason that I could put a name to, but it's far from the first time in my life that I've needed it.

So I walked slowly round its stalwart trunk, that great girth of old sandstone which masses squarely upwards into the most supreme building that ever rooted on Dundee soil. Did they know, these stonemasons of 1460, what they were building? Did they work to someone's plan or did they feel their way up to the master mason's bidding? 'The whole composition is admirably bound together by a stair turret to the top on the northern side' wrote Ian Hannah. 'Composition' . . . a telling word, but whose composition, given that the profession of 'architect' was still some centuries off? Who first stroked his medieval chin, pointing to a corner of the first foundation square and said – 'a stair . . . there!' and then, 'that'll bind the whole thing together – admirably!' and then, aloud to his labouring squad of lesser masons: 'Hold it, boys, this corner needs to be reworked a bit, for the projecting stair turret . . . you'll have to do this bit again, like this,' and took a stick and drew in the mud, and one among the more truculent of his workforce swore that if he was spared there would be a singularly unflattering likeness of the master mason fixed into some discreet corner of an upper storey, if the whole tottering mass of the tower didn't attract the fearful disapproval of an angry God and bury them all in a monumental collapse.

With that kind of rummaging preoccupation in my head this autumn Saturday, I became slowly aware of an unearthly music, a far-off echo-y discordancy, vaguely familiar yet weird in its setting. At first it was only a distant infringement on my thoughts, but it persisted in its weirdness so that I finally interrupted my silent self by turning angrily on the source of the sound. But where was it? What was it? It paused. It began again, half-heard, so that I thought for a moment it was a sound-track from my medieval reverie, a troubadour ghost still playing. I shut down the reverie and listened hard to the music. Its source was not the tower but the far end of the Overgate Centre's shopping-mall. That grim tunnel was acting like a gramophone horn to the first of the morning's buskers. What I was hearing was 'The Bonnie Lass o Fyvie' played very hesitantly on a solo trombone.

I shuddered and headed for the nearest café where a window seat let me look on the back of the city churches with the Old Steeple at their far end, shadowed and hard-edged from here, and massive.

I have sat down my hypothetical teenager (remember him?) at this window seat, too, for I want him to see this. We are now in the Overgate as redefined by the 1960s redevelopment, the worst buildings in this town or any other as I see them, which may be unfair, but not very unfair. The sound of running water permeates the quiet conversations of a few cappuccino-and-doughnut customers, designer ambience, except that it isn't. The water piddles through the tackiest plastic fountain you have ever seen, until on the way out you notice there is another one in the window by the door. I will not have to point this out to my teenager because sound will be in his ear. He will turn round and (I hope – how I hope!) grimace. And at the sight of the grimace I will say this:

'Plasticity. The state of being plastic. Have you ever noticed that the word "plasticity" is the nearest thing in the English language to the expression (I have just invented) "plastic city"?'

That fountain is to the geysers of Iceland what the Overgate Centre is to the Old Steeple. In other words, they should not co-exist on the same planet. The brain which envisaged that plastic fountain (and somebody did! – somebody designed it, somebody made it, somebody offered it for sale and, most incredibly of all, somebody bought it) has its parallel organ in the collective wisdom which pronounced the death knell of the old Overgate and pronounced this as its worthy successor.

You see, hypothetical laddie, not for the first time in our history, we are in throes of reinventing ourselves, or rather, we are in the throes of reinventing wur ahld hame toon. All the purposes for which Dundee was built, for which it prospered and fought and faltered and boomed and faded again . . . all these purposes have long since withered, and you cannot sustain a city, even a small city, on purposelessness. And because that extinct series of purposes have all leaned towards the heaviest of industries, we are saddled with the wreckage such industries leave in their wake when they die or depart.

It is hardly the prettiest of legacies and we have added insults to its many injuries by building unwisely. You do not build skyscrapers on a hillside site. They wreck nature's profile, and the hillside profile is Dundee's best feature. Do you see what I'm getting at, hypothetical laddie? In the reinventing process we have summoned a handsome old ship home and called it tourism. But above all things, if you invite tourism into your midst, you must be worth looking at, you must be . . . well, bonnie. Bonnie Dundee, eh?' Look around you, laddie, look at this plasticity where we sit, look out of the window, look at everything you see, and tell me what you see that's bonnie, everything that you would be proud to show off to a tourist coming curiously into our midst. The Ahld Steeplie, right?

And here's another discrepancy between what we have been and what (it seems) we have to be now. In the past we have manufactured things here and sent whatever we've manufactured all over the world. Suddenly, we are doing the reverse. We're making nothing that is distinctively ours, and we're inviting the rest of the world to come and see us, manufacturing tourism. But wouldn't you say that we have forgotten the first rule of manufacturing, the one which built all our good eras and prosperities? Have we not forgotten the product? The *Discovery* is sublime, but she does not amount to a tourist industry, and given that she suffers like the rest of us from having our waterfront cut off from the city centre, does that not suggest to you that we're blowing a tourist trumpet before we've learned how to play it?

We have a bonnie setting. We must become bonnie ourselves, or at least as bonnie as the ingrained psychology of our industrial heritage will permit. The easiest way (and it's all relative – none of it is easy) is to remove the worst of our self-sown carbuncles and make the most of what we have; what we have, that is, that nobody else has. To wit . . . our landscape, our Ahld Steeplie, and our waterfront. We begin here, and we begin by building, or rather rebuilding the one thing which will win over the hearts and minds of our own people, the one thing which will throw our own weight behind the idea of our own reinvention, the one thing which will give ourselves back what it is we miss most *and* provide fit accompaniment to the Old Steeple . . . the Overgate.

You are too young, my hypothetical friend, to know the pull of that single street. But it was in its own modest way, the heart of the city, and it is nothing more than the most praiseworthy of characteristics that Dundee people should take such an unostentatious little street for its symbolic centrepiece. Part of it was just its own close-gathered intimacy. Its scale suited us. Part of it was the overlording Steeple, which (along with Cox's Stack) is the only architectural grandeur we proclaim. It is not just sentiment, not just nostalgia (though both play their part) which harks us back to the Overgate's old sounds and smells. The heart of today's Dundee has slewed eastwards, wallowing uncertainly somewhere around the Murraygate, adrift in its own unconfident corpus, when all the time it should be feeding from our one great focal point, our one masterpiece of individuality, last bastion of our medievalality, the Ahld Steeplie hersel, and of course she's female. Let the *Discovery* be the catalyst by all means, for she's beautiful while the Steeple's just braw, and she makes a better play on words. But the great square tower is the mast we should nail our true colours to, and (as I hope I have now demonstrated, young laddie) our true colours are the shades of mud, that mud-stone which was our own beginning.

What we call the beginning is often the end
And to make an end is to make a beginning.
The end is where we start from.

You see? I told you T.S. Eliot was Dundee's kind of poet. Our beginning is so crucial to all our ends. And the end of Dundee's one-thousand-year stone-built era is the beginning we should honour as we seek to reinvent ourselves.

Dundee's relationship with its past is obsessive, our appetite for old photographs practically gluttonous. The past is what we prefer. The present, where it has usurped the built fabric of the past, is the wrong colour, the wrong shape, the wrong size, and the wrong frame of mind. It has served us less well. When we look at it, we do not see ourselves in it. We see ourselves in the mud-coloured walls. When we listen to its rhythms we don't hear Jeemy Shand's confident swinging and undemonstrative accordion, we hear a wailing, faltering trombone or something just as unearthly. The past was when Dundee made its name and could live up to it. When sepia photographs changed to colour, the colour of Dundee's walls didn't change at all.

The faces of the past are the ones we own up to, the streets of the past are the ones we inhabit in our minds. We know in our heart of hearts that one day the Overgate will rise again, that one day we will wake up to find Dock Street a waterfront again with traffic on one side of the road and ships on the other. That is the Dundee we fold into countless books and booklets, the Dundee we exhibit tirelessly, the Dundee which adorns our pub walls, the Dundee whose company we care to keep.

My parents belonged to a different Dundee. A war had come and gone and those of us born on this side of it were not coloured by it. I grew up expecting more than my parents and they encouraged my expectations. And when their city began to be demolished, I saw (an uncomprehending teenager myself, mind) the shape of a bright and glassy future. But I have grown, and I have adopted the mantle of my parents, regret, and I have started to see myself only in the mud-coloured stones.

Look in this shop window. See how many of these paintings show – lovingly – the Overgate that was, the High Street with the Pillars intact, the Vaults, the Hawkhill, the Dock Street that had wee trains running along its seaward side. There is nothing of what has replaced them.

What is gone is gone, but luckily we have painters in our midst whose muse is the past. They have an almost limitless source material to work and re-work, because from the nineteenth-century dawn of the photographic age, Dundee embraced the camera and its works more enthusiastically than most places. Folk were aye stopping other folk in the street with the words:

'Stand there a minute. Eh'll tak yer pho'ie.'

And now that it is no longer possible to photograph that particular Dundee – because it has been demolished, disfigured, discoloured and disappointed by the new order, and streetwise bairns have put socks and trainers on their bare feet – new generations of painters have begun to paint the old photographs. Playwrights have turned the old photographs into plays, and all manner of people from academics to poets to tourism promoters have begun to scratch away at the surface of the old photographs in search of Dundee's misplaced soul.

You will remember, perhaps, that I said I had a plan to set the Steeple and the Overgate to rights. It is time, I think, to unveil it, time to call up the ghost of the one man to emerge from the pack of Victorian improvers with the highest of ideals and a vision which was at times blinding, a vision with which, had it not been for the unsavoury intervention of the First World War, he would have astonished Dundee and the world.

Chapter Twelve

The Vision Splendid

So it is not exactly my plan. I have merely hitched it to the cause of my crusade. I have embraced it with the missionary fervour of a disciple from the moment I first saw a faded souvenir of its existence foot-noted in a museum exhibit. The exhibit is that toy-town-scale model of pre-Victorian Dundee which so enthrals visitors and saddens natives as much as it fascinates them. My own child-wide eyes used to marvel at it without so much as a glance at the photograph in a corner of its glass case. My mind played Dinky Toy games in its streets and that was the height of any ambition I ever held for the most charismatic museum-piece in town. I don't even remember if the photograph was there then, but it's there now and it begs for a wider audience. When I see it now, which is often (I drink from it, an inspiratory well), I want to make an enlargement the size of the Old Steeple, a one-photograph exhibition, and unfurl it from the roof of that Overgate Centre wall which cold-shoulders its way into that space where once the Overgate proper met the High Street. It must hang from that particular wall because that is where the miracle will stand, or at least it's where it stood in the visionary mind of the one civic genius Dundee ever accommodated – James Thomson.

Thomson was from Edinburgh, but he joined the staff of the burgh surveyor's department in Dundee around 1870 as a young man. He translated the Improvements Act of 1871 in a manner unique among his contemporaries, and his experiences working on post-Improvement Act projects were coloured by the breadth of his vision, a relentless optimism in the face of much scepticism, and a compassion for the working classes of downtrodden Dundee.

Among his countless contributions to the well-being of the city, as city architect and city engineer, was one tossed in almost as an aside in his landmark *Report on the Development of the City* to Dundee Town Council in 1918. He could do that, throw a fully matured idea into the air, plucked out of the most unlikely and barely related chrysalis. At one point he is writing about his ambition to 'approach the standard of perfection which should be the aim in the comprehensive plan of development' (and when did you last hear a council official plead with his councillors to aim for perfection?) by recommending a civilised proportion of parkland be incorporated in new housing developments. The next moment he slips in a one-paragraph recommendation, in the midst of which is 'my' photograph. It reads:

> Ideal conditions in the provision of small open spaces for the central densely populated areas are impossible of attainment, whether for ornament or as playgrounds for children, and the Council should take advantage of every opportunity to secure bright spots of colour, however small, in the busy and crowded areas. Albert Square and the grounds of the City Churches are typical of what might be done.

So far, so very mundane, but then there is the bombshell, and the photograph.

> An example of how such an opportunity may soon present itself in the very heart of the city is here shown.
>
> This drawing illustrates what could be done in the embellishment of a part of the central area, and incidentally, it also shows a possible scheme for the removal of the old Town House to a new site. This scheme would materially appreciate the value of the Corporation properties in the new business square, and at the same time provide a further attractive open space for the centre of the city in front of the Caird Hall.

My 'photograph' has proved to be a crude representation of a large architect's drawing. What I had not known when I first asked at the museum for a copy of the photograph was that the original was one of a series of huge watercolours. I was shown them by the City Archivist, Iain Flett. They were stashed away in the far corner of a storeroom under the Caird Hall where the only light is electric and the predominant colour is brown. It is a quiet and musty fate for such daring. Occasionally they surface for exhibitions which astound the populace with might-have-beens, when a few more eyes and minds are opened wider by the name of James Thomson.

But 'my' watercolour was not among them.

Iain Flett thought someone at the university might know, and cheerfully telephoned him on my behalf. The man at the university thought it was on an office wall in Building Control, but George McGilvary, whose office it was, proved to be on holiday. I was given a phone number. When he returned I phoned, explained the purpose behind the enquiry again, only to be told that the watercolour on his wall was the 'wrong' one. It showed the Town House all right, but on its original site with a garden and fountain where the later picture proposed to re-site the Town House. He was not at all sure where the one I was looking for was, but he would make some inquiries.

I was beginning to realise that the name of James Thomson had an almost magical cachet among his heirs. Not once did my inquiries meet with anything other than enthusiastic co-operation, no hint of the 'I've got-better-things-to-do' impatience I had half-expected.

It took two more weeks, more phone calls, more intermittent inquiries, then one more phone call to Jack Searle, then chief planning officer of Tayside Region. I ran through the routine again, concluding: 'I rather hope that the watercolour is on your wall.'

'It is indeed,' he replied, and I punched the air with the hand which wasn't holding the phone. A few days later, I was shown into his office and came face to face with 'the vision splendid', as I would come to think of it.

I appreciate that 'finding' one architect's drawing which was never actually lost is hardly the search for the Holy Grail, but from the day I first saw the museum photograph of it, it had lodged in my mind as a symbol of Dundee's possibilities. Now that I had the whole watercolour to linger over, I was more impressed than ever with the mind which lay behind it, a mind prepared to play chess gambits with the city's set pieces to achieve the nearest thing to a state of architectural grace that Dundee was ever likely to muster.

It is that mind which I have harnessed to the bidding of The Plan.

The Plan is sublimely simple. First demolish the Overgate Centre. It has no place in what follows. It was a mistake, and a hideous one at that. Own up, flatten it and the morbid dark grey office tower which bellows its forlorn 'To Let' message across the city centre to the disinterest of the lieges.

Second, reinstate the Overgate along its old line. But as nothing else survives from the old warren of streets and alleys which once prevailed there, it should perhaps be born again as a one-sided street of town centre houses and small shops, and contemplating the Old Steeple and its acolyte churches set in one of those spots of garden colour which James Thomson prized so highly.

Third, rebuild the Town House, as Thomson had envisaged it, with the Pillars reinstated as Dundee's pre-eminent meeting-place, and with a new garden square to the east of it.

The Town House must be built in our own stone, the fronts of the Overgate shops likewise. I know where to get it. Demolish the Coffin Mill, and in the process allow one more spot of garden and parkland colour into a corner of the city which has shivered too long in that sinister shadow.

Now step back and look at what we have achieved for the purposes of putting a spring in the step of the natives and galvanising this tourism we so covet. We have liberated the Old Steeple, which is its due, given it back the dignity its uniqueness demands. We have resurrected the Overgate, the supreme gesture we can make to the hearts and minds of ourselves. We have rebuilt and greatly improved the setting of William Adam's 1731 Town House (it was formerly only visible from one side; now, like a good sculpture, it can be seen from all four). We have honoured James Thomson by demonstrating the timelessness of his vision. We have in the Pillars a building hailed in its day as the finest Town House in Scotland to put to use in a way which will serve both ourselves and our visitors. It will tell Dundee's story, it will welcome tourists with a degree of panache and hospitality to make other tourist information centres pale. And it will put on permanent display the mind and the spirit of James Thomson. The seventy-fifth anniversary of his death is in 2002. That should be time enough.

The irony of what will be an ambitious civic project by anyone else's standards, is that in Thomson's terms it emerges apparently as a throwaway, no more than a means to an end. He built the Caird Hall in the years 1914-21 and craved the space to the north of it for a public square with civic buildings on its east and west flanks. The Pillars stood in his way. It was in the nature of the Victorians, all reformers with Victorian roots, to clear away the obstructive past in pursuit of the new enlightenment. But even Thomson hesitated over the Adam Town House, and its focal point Pillars. In the end he did not remove it and it wasn't until 1930 that it was carted away in the face of one more public outrage, neither the first nor the last in Dundee.

But Thomson had grander designs. Contemporary drawings show a Christopher Wren-ish dome peering into the City Square from somewhere above and behind the Caird Hall. It was there, on a reclaimed site on the waterfront, that Thomson dared his utmost. Unconstrained by existing streets and buildings, and relishing the south-facing slope of the sun-flooded Firth of Tay, he dreamed neo-classical dreams, a monumentally palatial new City Hall with formal gardens flanked by an esplanade which in his wildest unfulfilled fantasy stretched from Invergowrie to Broughty Ferry.

So was that his motivation for sliding the Town House across the road and opening sightlines towards the Caird Hall, knowing that the spectral dome hinted at in his drawings was also, on his agenda at least, the crown of his Civic Hall? And how like him to have a vision for the displaced masterpiece too, while in pursuit of a vision of his own.

I wonder how infectious his enthusiasm was in his own time? I wonder because in the scratching of his surface almost seventy years after his death I feel curiously drawn to the daring so evident in his repertoire of ideas, infected at first sight by the apparently casual skill of the Town House project. I have a fond image in my mind's eye of the purpling faces of Dundee councillors as he unfurled the details of his development report of 1918, perhaps uncovering one huge water-colour after another; one bemused councillor after another wrestling with the preposterousness of the proposition before them. Did they rejoice at the genius in their midst, at the possibilities laid before them of elevating Dundee's status in the eyes of the nation to a city befitting its unrivalled site? Or did they think that their scatterbrained city architect had finally slipped his tenuous moorings, finally dragged the anchor of his sanity and drifted off helplessly and beyond control out into the treacherous currents of the Firth? Doomed? However they felt about it all, Thomson's grand design never progressed beyond the frame of his own watercolours, and the city and its city architect ended their formal relationship in a sad and unworthy row about the amount of money Thomson had overspent on a council house heating scheme.

You would think he might have died a bitter man, but his ambition never faltered. He retained some consultancy capacity after his retirement and spent it pursuing the same dreams. I went in search of my man, and found at least something of him in the Wellgate Library's obituary books. He was seventy-five when he died in November 1927. The photograph shows an Anthony Eden-ish figure in a soft hat and starched collar. The circumstances of his death could not be more poignant, for he collapsed in a corridor of the Caird Hall, 'the building with which his name will ever be associated' in the words of the obituary writer.

'His fondest hope and expressed desire was to have the Caird Hall Square completed "in his time" and at the moment of death he was engaged on some of the minor details relating to the scheme for the east wing of the building. This was the purpose of his call at the City Chambers.'

The curiously formal journalism of the day then narrates the great man's last moments thus:

'A woman caller who awaited the Lord Provost saw him fall in the main corridor. She informed Lord Provost High and Mr S. G. Fraser with whom he was engaged at the moment, and they ran to Mr Thomson's assistance. Mr Thomson made a vain effort to speak but passed away in the arms of Mr Fraser.'

James Thomson was, according to the reporter, 'the creator of innumerable schemes to make Dundee the city beautiful' and he struggled through an uninspiring list . . . the construction of Perth Road, the introduction of trams . . . 'and in the erection of the cattle markets . . . and slaughterhouses, baths and hospitals, Mr Thomson took a leading part'.

But such was the city's confidence in James Thomson at the turn of the century that he became City Architect in 1904 and City Engineer two years later, at which point the reporter permits himself a poetic flourish.

'Mr Thomson was gifted with the vision splendid.'

And then:

'Long before Governments began to take town planning as a serious consideration he was thinking out schemes for a better and greater Dundee. He had the outlook of an idealist and a visionary, and planned not only for the present but for the future.

'In his efforts for the better housing of the people, Mr Thomson earned a national reputation . . . Dundee had houses building while other corporations were not beyond the stage of bickering over the buying of ground.

'There is no need for a monument to be erected in Dundee to the memory of James Thomson. Like Wren, it can be said of him:

' "If you seek any monument, look around."

'It is to be seen in the magnificent Caird Hall, which he designed and which was erected under his personal supervision; it will be seen more effectively when High Street area is cleared of its old buildings [aha! so he did seal the fate of the Town House!] and the Caird Hall Square which he has planned, comes into existence; it is to be found in the corporation housing schemes which now dot the city and in many other works of civic undertaking.'

It was a deep breath James Thomson must have drawn before he pronounced an astounding list of prophecies at his retirement speech, prophecies which, from this distance at least, range from the inspired to the insane, but that was the nature of a truly remarkable beast. The obituary intones:

'The outer ring road of the Kingsway will be one of the greatest thoroughfares and the finest boulevard in the country.

'The Tay Road Bridge will be a reality. He had first proposed the idea in 1914 and it was a plank of his 1918 development report. As well, perhaps, that he did not live to see the almost bankrupt city turn down two road bridge schemes in 1929 – a high level bridge at £3 million and a low level one at £1 million which the Government thought so modest it offered 80 per cent grants, and still the city couldn't afford them . . . on such rocks the vision splendid is apt to splinter.

'Newport, Wormit and Tayport will be annexed to Dundee and the river front to the east of East Newport will be an industrial centre of Dundee. Ye Gods!

'The Esplanade would reach from Invergowrie to Broughty Ferry.

'The Caird Hall Square will be completed.

'Overgate Improvement will be completed.

'Earl Grey and King William Docks will be filled in and form the site of a civic centre fronting what will ultimately be a central railway station.

'Dundee will be practically a smokeless city, central heating being general and labour-saving houses will become the rule rather than the exception.'

And finally . . .

'To his great capacity as a man of affairs, Mr Thomson united a most attractive and kindly personality.'

James Thomson – 1852 to 1927, the visionary splendid.

'Suppose,' I said to Alfie that night in The Pillars, before we moved on to the Mercantile (which is where we do our really serious philosophising) 'suppose we do actually rebuild the Town House and suppose our Thomson-less city faithers are so taken with it that they decide to flick through Thomson's shopping list again . . . '

'Eh'm readin yur mind, Jimmy. Your wonderin . . . whu' if we tak a turn tae wursels an examine the outrage wuv perpetrati' on the site o es greatest endeavours – the wah'erfron?'

'Right. You know, an Eh know, Alfie, wur road bridge's shite.'

'Too right, Jimmy. A shitey bridge, and it breenges intae the middle o the toon, an it shouldnae. So . . . '

'So, Alfie, meh drunken, drouthie cronie, we remind wursels that James Thomson's bridge was oot beh the railway bridge, mimicking its lang, lang curve, so the bridge'd be bonnier beh far, and . . . '

'An it's be'er plissed beh far 'n' ah! Comes ashore beh the airport, handy fur the Keengsway for ahbdy as wahnts tae go north or west an disnae wahnt tae guddle aboo in Dundee – where, beh the wey, we dinnae wahnt them tae guddle aboo' either!'

'An the greatest prehz o ah, Alfie, meh boozed-up amigo, is that we get wur wah'erfront back!'

'Eh, Jimmy, we get it back, but whu are we daein wi it, now

148

tha it's wur ain again? Yer surely no fahin fur that neo-classical keech . . . '

It was not a question, but rather a summation of many previous conclusions Alfie and I have drawn on the subject of built Dundee, and Thomson's definition of it in particular. 'Keech' was a mite unworthy of the Civic Hall with the Wren dome, for the design was wondrously wrought, formidably dared, and – as Alfie and I see it not as much a specific ambition Thomson nurtured but an example of the kind of daring which Dundee's desperate plight demanded. I wonder.

I wonder what Thomson really had in his mind when he confronted his adopted city with a project so idealistic that even he must have sensed it was more or less unattainable. But was that the point? If he presented it, then pulled back from it, would the town council in its profound relief be only too willing to hasten the progress of his real dreams? (And I wonder if the presumptious acquisition of the north Fife shore for industry was another such device!)

His Civic Hall was breathtaking, but was it Dundee? Did he really expect approval for a municipal palace while the height of most Dundonians' ambitions was an inside toilet? The Dundee Social Union Report of 1905 had conducted a survey of 6,500 Dundee households and found that 31 per cent did not have the use of a toilet shared by less than twelve people; and that 72 per cent of the population lived in houses with either one or two bedrooms. No one knew these figures and what they represented on the ground more intimately than James Thomson, and no one was more committed to the cause of decent housing for the working classes. But no one was more committed at the same time to making as much of a silk purse as he could out of the sow's ear of a city where he toiled. Think this big, he was saying with his Civic Hall fantasia, and anything is possible. He designed not an architectural ambition like the Caird Hall and City Square, but a catalyst to jolt civic thinking into a new era, or so it seems to me. He would know as well as anyone that Dundee was a working city with its roots in the sea, that a municipal palace for a landfall would amount to a serious misrepresentation of Dundee character.

I suspect that Thomson was too shrewd and too sensitive a human being to override the character of the people for whom he did so much, the people whose interests he so relentlessly pursued.

Yet look what we have now, instead, on that very site – a spell-bindingly tragic wasteland hinged to a hopelessly mis-sited road bridge, a sordid off-the-peg municipal tower block, a casino (just what we always wanted), and a hotel with all the architectural hall-marks of Torness, Hunterston and Sizewell B. And a swimming-pool only mildly mitigated by its stitched-on afterthought canopy. The whole lot is so appallingly alien to real people on two legs that our only means of reaching our beloved and birthright waterfront is to thole half-mile detours through glass-walled corridors on stilts, pos-sibly the most hostile pedestrian environment mankind has ever taken the trouble to invent. Just as Billy Connolly has pointedly argued that only a celibate could have invented the rhythm method, only a dullard with a chauffeur could have invented Dundee's air-borne corridors. In the face of all that, what Alfie declaimed as 'that neo-classical keech' is a fair approximation of Paradise.

But if Thomson was as attuned to the needs and aspirations of Dundee people as I suspect, he would know that (a) they liked their waterfront nibbling at the streets of the town, and (b) they would be much more amenable to the dignifying of familiar landmarks in their midst rather than a purpose-built masterpiece which came between them and their river. Here is an introductory paragraph in a 1910 sub-mission to the town council *before* the Caird Hall, the City Chambers and the City Square were begun, and when the decaying but charis-matic old shapes of the Vaults still thronged the space behind the Town House. Here – I think – is the real strategy of James Thomson, implied if not spelled out:

To the Dundee Town Council

GENTLEMEN,

In the consideration of a Scheme of Central Improvements the Council are compelled to have in view the provision of a site for the erection at some near or distant date of a City Hall and Municipal Buildings sufficient for the needs and worthy of a city of the size and importance of Dundee, and they are further presumably bound to allow for the retention of the Old Town House on its present site, which, by the way, is not a happily selected one. [He is loading the dice already. At the beginning of the sentence the Council 'are compelled' – no shred of doubt – but later they are 'presumably bound', a clear invitation to doubt. Maybe we can shift the damned thing!] Any Scheme is, therefore, to a large extent, influenced by these considerations, and, while the suggestion hereinafter made as to a site for the proposed Civic Centre materially simplifies the proposals for improvements, yet the position of the present Town House exerts a certain restraint in the lay-out of the High Street as well as of the area on the south, [excuse me while I slip some italics around Thomson's phrase] *and thus the plan cannot pretend to the perfection which might have obtained had the present building not existed.* It will be obvious that if a sufficiently spacious site can be found for the Civic Centre not abutting on High Street and still in its immediate vicinity, the whole Scheme of Improvements is relieved of much difficulty; and if a satisfactory arrangement can be made by the Council with the Harbour Trustees for space at the Harbour, substantial progress may be said to have been made with regard to one of the most important, if not the most urgent, parts of the Scheme.

That submission includes an architect's drawing of a widened High Street and Overgate with the Town House *in situ* and a formal garden with fountain on the very site where, a few years later, James Thomson had, in his mind's eye at least, transported the Town House. Both visions, incidentally, thought nothing of sweeping away one of Dundee's oldest houses, where General Monk moved in after he captured the town in 1651, but it was the besetting sin of all Victorian reformers that conservation did not darken their agenda. Thomson, who would have rubbled Monk's temporary HQ and the Town House, if he could have got away with it, incorporated the vile Royal Arch into his Civic Hall designs, presumably for no other reason than that it was a product of his own era. It hardly matched his own standards of aesthetics. The Overgate Centre finally accounted for the old house in 1966, and conservation was still not on the agenda, although in Edinburgh it had been avidly practised for decades and flourished alongside madcap sixties redevelopment.

When James Thomson casually introduced his 1918 proposal for a re-sited Town House, I think he had neatly concluded the height of his realistic ambition for central Dundee, and I think it was his real stroke of genius. There was his Caird Hall, there was his City Square with its flanking buildings accommodating council chamber and offices and, with the Town House transplanted to a site which showed it off to infinitely greater advantage, there was the sightline he craved so that there was light and space, formality and planning about his endeavours. *And* he could be seen to be doffing his cap reverentially to the architecture of an earlier era. He was giving the people of Dundee dignity in their midst rather than grandeur stashed aloofly away beyond the bulwark of the Caird Hall. It was complete, and that ghost of a dome which peers over the roof of the Caird Hall in his artwork for the Caird Hall–City Square scheme? That was him making mischief, and hinting to the town council that if they cared to dream *really* big dreams, then he was their man for that job too.

And so, we have it in our power now, and preferably between 1996 and 2002, to build his afterthought that wasn't an afterthought, to put the Town House back into the landscape of our midst, and put the Pillars back as the focal point of all of us. We should do it.

That other Pillars, which is the Crichton Street howff with a model of the Town House where others might hang a Guinness sign, was the muse we invoked – Alfie and I – by virtue of the fact that the streetlight and the rain conspired to illuminate that model of the Pillars suspended above the pub door in a way that made us give it a second glance. And, to answer Alfie's disrespectful question, I'm not falling for that neo-classical municipal palace. But it all begs one more hypothetical.

Alfie duly begged it.

'So wuv realigned wur bridge, Jimmy.'

'Right.'

'We've flattened Faulty Tower there now that the regional cooncil's migrated to Forfar.'

'Right.'

'Wuv told Reo Stakis tae move on an tak es cuboid hotel and es casino wi im.'

'Right.'

'Wuv dug up ah they trashy bridge approaches and cahd doon the wahkweys in the skeh.'

'Right.'

'So we're back tae a fla' bu' oh grund wi nothin atween the Cairdie an the wah'er?'

'Right.'

'An wur no buildin neo-classical municipal palaces.'

'Right.'

'So . . . wur buildin *whu'* exactly?'

'Eh've been wondrin aboo' tha' for some time.'

'Eh wiz afraid ye mightuv been. So . . . ?'

'So, Alfie, meh wise architectural consultant and sage, ken how wuv jist buhl' the Toon Hoose tha' husnae been seen fur mair nor 60 year?'

'Right. Hehpothe'ically speakin, uv coorse.'

'Uv coorse. Well, stuhll dealin in hehpothe'ics, uv coorse, Eh'm in favour o buhldin back the ahld feel o the pliss, an . . . oh, ken how ahld Lerwick an ahld Stromness wade into the wah'er . . . well ahld Dundee did that afore. An ken whu' i wuz ye hud tae wahk through tae get there?'

Alfie frowned, scratched his head, drained a dreg, then, as if a leerie had just passed with pole poised, Alfie's face lit.

'The bloody Vaults! You *bugger*! You wahn' the Vaults back! You bugger!'

Two 'you buggers' from Alfie in one breath was praise indeed.

Why the Vaults? Three reasons.

One. It gets harder and harder with every passing reformist decade to gain any sense at all of that Dundee which grew instinctively out from its old core, feeling its way along old travellers' roads, throwing up a courtyard here, a kirk there, cutting lanes from its new trading centre to its waterfront which it must always cling to – must, because to distance *living* Dundee from the waterfront is to deny the reason for the city's very existence. Our own era is the first in one thousand years of our history to push us back from our own waterfront. We owe it to ourselves to have that fundamental restored. The Vaults were the old means by which it was achieved, an eighteenth-century conclave which wound down through wynds and closes from the High Street to the harbour. A caption in one of Dundee's countless publications of old photographs intones the familiar tale: 'It generally fell into disrepair and disrepute as the once grand eighteenth-century town houses were subdivided.' They were one more casualty of James Thomson's vision splendid, but if we put the Greenmarket back on its original site under the back of the Caird Hall, let some of the water back into the south side of the new market square, and build the Vaults or something very like it, on a waterfront site, we would be turning back an iniquitous tide which has been as contemptuous of Thomson's vision for Dundee as the Victorians were for medieval Dundee. We know now what the Victorians did not – the worth of heritage and the techniques of conservation and rebuilding the past for its own sake.

Two. The visual impact of old stone houses on our waterfront would delight Dundee people and these new legions of tourists to whom we wish to appeal and be appealing. Building new houses instead of new roads in the heart of the city would establish an invigorating precedent.

Three. A born-again Vaults would be a declaration of intent and a pointed rebuke to all the generations of demolitioners who have razed our past to all too low a common denominator.

Alfie heard all this in silence, which is rare in Alfie, but after his enthusiastic greeting of the principle, I sensed his attention wandering here and there and, knowing Alfie, I sensed his silence was building up to something. He suddenly said:

'Ken whu Eh wuz, wundrin?'

'When wuz Eh goin tae get up aff meh bumbuleerie an beh a roond?' I offered.

'That 'n' ah, now you mention it, but say that had been a fullum when the Ahld Mannie Thomson dehd in thon chap's airums . . .'

'A fullum, Whu' . . . like John Wayne?'

'Exactly. In the fullums they aye get tae speak thur deathbed speeches. Eh wuz wundrin tae mehsel, whu' wuz e trehin to say?'

'Oh, tha's a good ain, Alfie. Eh think wur awa tae the Mercantile afore we tackle tha ain.'

'Fair enough, Jimmy, but it's stuhll your roond.'

The Mercantile, apotheosis of Dundee's howffs, cless in a gless. A corner seat, the bar tranquil in the midwinter midweek mid-evening. Alfie contrived his best educated Edinburgh voice, and miraculously pronounces the last unspoken speech of James Thomson. What he said was this, croakily, as if it was a fullum:

'If I had known it was to come to this, I would have written these things down to pass them on. But it seems there is not time.

'The streets. The people. You must give the streets back to the people. This is the drabbest era the people have ever known. We have pushed back the walls a bit. We have let in a little more sun. But it is not enough.

'This city – your city, for it is not even mine, except by adoption and the hospitality of all of you – is twice blessed: it is on the sunniest of Scotland's shores and it inhabits a south-facing . . . sun-facing . . . hillside. Yet there is so little sunlight in our streets.

'We blot it out with too much smoke and too many walls too close together. The people are housed in buildings from which they can only view the monotony of paved streets or the dullness of factory walls. What is built was mostly built too hastily and too poorly, and with too little regard for the inhabitants. For that matter they were also built with too little regard for architecture and for the architect's two great elusives – form and light.

'Month after month when I came here, I walked these streets. They were the meanest streets I had ever seen. Yet their situation was the fairest. That cannot be right, I told myself, for it seemed to me that the people wore the clothes of the mean streets, not the clothes of their fair situation. I determined early, that should the fruits of my labours ever ripen to the extent that I was able to bring the strength of my resolve to bear on their lot, I should put form and light into their midst, clean air and sunlight, so that they might wear the clothes of the fair situation.

'For there will come a day when the great industries have faltered and fled, and Dundee must trade on its fair situation. It will not do then to have mean streets and natives who wear the clothes of the mean streets. We have made a beginning. Build beautifully, by my example, think of transforming the mean streets with form and light. Most important of all, for what is to come, beautify the waterfront, beautify our central spaces, for it is in these two theatres of our city that tourism (for that is how we will earn our trade and do not scorn or underestimate its potency) will want to linger. See that it finds us beautified and hospitable. See that we present the fair face. See that there is sunlight enough to play on it.'

'Good, Alfie. Eh'm dreh. It's your roond.'

Chapter Thirteen

Poet and Tragedian

My dearly beloved readers. – I have decided to set down before you, and in response to the oft-repeated question wheresoever I have performed my entertainments, a little of the secrecies which attend my craft. Ah, but, I hear you say, surely you have two crafts, and of course you are correct, for I am both weaver (and a good one, so I have been told by those who have cause to celebrate my work at the loom) *and* poet. But it is to the craft of poet I allude, for it is that which so beguiles and intrigues you, My Dear Friends, and commands all my waking hours.

Let me show you the simplest facet of my techniques. In one sense it has to do with the weaving of cloths, and in that same sense my former craft befits me well for my present craft, the craft of the poet. I stitch one word to another. Then, and at every opportunity, if it is a felicitous stitching, I will repeat it as often as possible so that it recurs in my work with predictable regularity and you will look on it fondly as a friend; like the chorus of the best songs, but more subtly placed. It is my great gift, and I dare say there are more people alive today who know more of my stitchings than they know lines of Burns.

The silvery Tay – that is my most felicitous stitching. It is doubly felicitous for it occurs in my best line:

The Tay, the Tay, the silvery Tay

It is fair to say (and many have, for a poet like myself has his detractors since he is much misunderstood) that the poem which begins thus is less sound, less well formed, sprung with a lesser tension from the second line onwards. Aha, but what a first line! Think of all the great poems which spring unbidden to the lips because we know the first line for its felicity and falter beyond it (if we know anything of what follows at all). To wit:

Earth has not anything to show more fair
The curfew tolls the knell of parting day
I wandered lonely as a cloud
Wee sleekit cowerin timorous beastie

To that stock I modestly contribute a pinch of my own.

The Tay, the Tay, the silvery Tay

Do you see what I am getting at here, My Dear Readers? If you have a great line, put it in first. There is no point in a great line buried. If you have a great line, let it turn heads, let it leave your reader a-gasp from the first. You have him then! It matters not that you have nothing else to say, or at least no inspired means of expressing what you have to say (for most poets have recourse to the remorselessly workaday for the greater body of their works a poem too replete with great lines would be as indigestible as too rich a pudding and I for one have scattered my great lines but thinly, the better to show them off). See, My Great Friends, is it not true that you forgive my unfelicity for the sake of the one great line which drew you to the poem in the first place? Perhaps I should not be giving away a poet's secrets with such recklessness, but I am characterised (I have heard it said by the perspicacious that my work is likewise characterised!) by my generosity of spirit.

The greatest honour that can befall a poet is not a Laureate-ship or a golden guinea (welcome as these are, My Dear Friends). It is the acclaim of his fellows. It is the lifting of his own lines off the page and into the realm of the workaday language of the people. The greatest feeling I know, My Very Dear Friends, is to be standing by that great river which is the hallmark of our city, and there to chance upon some complete stranger oblivious of my identity and to hear him remark to the lady at his side 'Ah, the Tay, the Tay . . .' and the fact that he utters the name twice is my unutterable pride and joy, my insatiable delight. If she should then respond 'the silvery Tay!' I could scarce forbear to reveal myself, such was the bursting gratification in my breast. But the divine inspiration under which I write, and which compels my hand (as it has done since that startling day in 1877 of which you are doubtless familiar as it is detailed in the much-quoted brief autobiography which prefaces my *Poetic Gems*), is also a formidable restrainment, and I habitually walk on with a generous smile, a cordial 'Good day to you' and a pointed doffing of my hat in the lady's direction.

How I love the ring of that profound monosyllable, 'Tay'! Wherever I travel, whether it be London, New York or (famously!) Balmoral, intent on the presentment of humble lines to Her Most Gracious Majesty, the sonorities of 'Tay'! are rarely far from my mind and lie unspoken on my lips but briefly. How well it has served my Muse, and how it resounds within me as a heartbeat must.

So it was that I came to write my proclamation of love for that noblest of all Nature's thoroughfares, 'The Silvery Tay', but My Dear Friends and Loyal Readers, it will surely intrigue you to learn that when the divine inspiration settled its cloak about my shoulders and bade me write such a poem, it provided no title. I simply dipped my pen in ink and wrote the first two words I must write: 'The Tay'. No! That is not the truth! I rebuke myself! I first wrote 'The River Tay' but the rhythm of its speech (and always I write for the line to be spoken, for an unspoken poem has all its resonances dulled) was ungainly on my ear and I had determined that this poem must open with a clarion of felicity. Besides, I scorned myself – a second rebuke! – we who know the privilege of abode on Tay's shore never refer to her as River Tay (that is a stranger's appellation!) but as the more hearty 'The Tay' which intimacy allows. One deft pen stroke expunged the offending line and I began again writing the first two *true* words I must write: 'The Tay'.

What force moves a poet's hand, Dear Readers, and what counter-force commands him to pause? I do not have the answers to such questions for all that I contemplate them often. Save that the answers embrace that which is Divine Inspiration and which commanded me to write on that startling day of 1877, when you and I, Reader and Poet, began our betrothal. Happy, startling day! Now, with the words 'The Tay' written out on the page, the counter-force stayed my hand and, having insisted on pause, permitted the moving force to command anew. 'The Tay' it commanded again and, while questioning the repetition in my mind, I wrote it out as bidden even as I questioned. I read aloud, 'The Tay, the Tay . . .' and oh how the rhythm of it rang in me! Here was my clarion, or at least its first sonorities. I sensed the line was unfinished, and bent myself to its completion with hitherto untasted relish. Sweet endeavour!

The chief felicity of the uncompleted line was its simple repetition. To say it once is merely to identify the scene. To say it twice is to fix the scene as the subject and implies admiration of the remorselessness of the river's motion as it sweeps past the city. Yet it is always present for as fast as it empties itself the sea fills it from the east and there is a felicitous betrothal of waters. All that is contained, albeit implicitly, in these two resonating syllables of the clarion: 'The Tay, the Tay'.

Dear Readers, Friends, permit me a small digression with my greatest line uncompleted. You will doubtless be aware of my visit to New York, America, in the year 1887 on board the beautiful steamer *Circassia*, a very pleasant voyage for a fortnight at sea, and while I was quite a favourite amongst the passengers, and displayed my histrionic abilities to their delight, I received no remuneration for so doing (but I was well pleased with the diet I received). During my stay in New York with a Dundee man, I tried occasionally to get an engagement from theatre and music hall proprietors, but alas! twas all in vain, for they all told me they didn't encourage rivalry. Thus, I was dispirited in my endeavours to repeat the felicity of simple repetition in a descriptive poem of that city. For, when I had first written down the words 'New York, New York', I saw again that (if the sonorities are appropriate) there is great power in the device. I was moved to create

a poem worthy of performance in the city itself, but so unaccommo-
dating were the theatre proprietors that I cried 'Fie!' on them and the
divine inspiration which had attended the poem's opening syllables
moved off. For although I wrestled anxiously, it is a tricky name to
rhyme and the only rhyme which ultimately served me well, I
reserved for the last verse, and it may be deemed to concisely reflect
my feelings towards the Americas.

And with regard to New York and the sights I did see,
One street in Dundee is more worth to me,
And believe me, the morning I sailed from New York
For Bonnie Dundee, my heart it felt as light as a cork.

Perhaps then the heart was not in the New York poem, but still I
sometimes turn up that page with the words 'New York, New York'
written there in my own hand, and I think it might amount to something. Perhaps it is not for me. Perhaps some later bard inspired by my
works to take up the pen himself – perhaps one of you, My Dear and
Loyal Friends and Readers – will make more of the idea and raise up
my spirit which looks on the words haplessly. Perhaps he will find a
great lyric beginning thus and, enjoying deserved success and fame,
credit the source of his inspiration which he has found in these pages,
and perhaps acknowledge it in remuneration which will be greatly
appreciated by the present writer as recipient. And that concludes my
small digression for which thanks, Dear Readers, for your indulgence.

My greatest poetic line lies where we left it on the second line of
the hand-written page (the first, you will remember, is the deletion
which contained the defiling word 'river'). And now I have a scene
for you, a portrait of the writer to set before you. It is winter in my
lodgings – it is *always* winter in my lodgings! – and my poet's wage is
as meagre as the gas mantle by which pale light I labour, crouched
across the table, daring my Muse not to desert me. The Tay, the Tay,
what now? A moth lodged in some crevice of the wall was suddenly
up at the mantle and I watched in horror as it alighted there and burst
into a single silver flame, then went out. That it should turn silver in
its last moment . . . silver . . . the silver Tay. I wrote the whole line –
The Tay, the Tay, the silver Tay. It was three-quarters of the way to
perfect. I do not know now by what means I arrived at the stroke of

near genius by which my mind took that simple word 'silver' and rendered it 'silvery', and it may well have been that it was nothing more than a copyist's error as I made a careful duplicate of my greatest line of poetry. But at some point in that uncharitable night's labour I wrote the whole line down for the first time as you are now so familiar with it, and I sat back and pronounced it perfect and retired and slept like a babe. In the grey Dundee morning which followed, it was as good as the night before, and I remembered the moth that had died in the cause of a line of poetry as I shall doubtless die myself, and there is no fitter way.

Now, my Dear Friends, since this *Book of Poems* which I have the honour of introducing to you this evening, will perhaps, be my last effort:

I earnestly hope the inhabitants of the beautiful city of Dundee
Will appreciate this little volume got up by me,
And when they read its pages, I hope it will fill their hearts with delight
While seated around the fireside on a cold winter's night;
And some of them, no doubt, will let a silent tear fall
In dear remembrance of

WILLIAM MCGONAGALL

Silvery it is, and so is any stretch of water which you must contemplate looking into the sun. The Tay from Dundee is east and south and west, and always you look at it against the sun, and silvery is what you get. But it took William McGonagall, poet and tragedian, to couple the two words and give them that spring of poetic felicity which bears endless repetition. From the moment he first stumbled on that coupling, he plugged it remorselessly, and the word 'Tay' hardly ever appeared solitarily in his entire oeuvre. Thus, he put his own poetry into the language of the people, and there are few enough poets who have ever achieved that. MacDiarmid held it as his highest ambition in his '*Second Hymn to Lenin*':

Are my poems spoken in the factories and fields
  In the streets o the toon?
Gin they're no, then I'm failin to dae
  What I ocht to ha' dune.

162

Then, two verses later:

> 'Haud on, haud on; what poet's dune that?
>   Is Shakespeare read,
> Or Dante or Milton or Goethe or Burns?'
>   – You heard what I said.

The answer, of course, to the question posed in the first line of that verse (not that MacDiarmid would have owned up to it) is William McGonagall. It is a cultural heresy – of course – to lob his name into any discussion of the great poets in the verse above and as far as I can deduce (and reading *between* McGonagall's lines is a crucial trick of the appreciation of his art) not even McGonagall laid claim to that kind of company. Critics squirm over him. How they must loathe the advent of the letter 'M' in their leaden compendiums of Scottish literary biography, or the second half of the nineteenth century, if it's a chronological tome, when they must either toil mightily to justify McGonagall's aberration in Stevenson's glorious era, or write him off with a practised sneer. It seems not to occur to them to omit him, presumably for fear of giving offence to the thousands who still buy McGonagall and still read him, year after year. Rather, they will insist on including him on their lists if only so that they can publicly disown him. The mightiest pen turned against him was perhaps Kurt Wittig, the German critic whose *The Scottish Tradition in Literature* is a monument to that genre:

> The *Poetic Gems* of The Great William McGonagall, poet and tragedian, and shabbiest of public house rhymesters, are still reprinted almost every year; and their continuing popularity would indeed be an interesting problem for a psychiatrist to study. It is not rock-bottom that we touch here, that would suggest something solid; with him poetry is irretrievably sunk in mire.

That's it. Included only for the satisfaction of an admittedly deft passing sideswipe. Wittig was writing in 1958, and thirty years later, Trevor Royle in the *Mainstream Companion to Scottish Literature* seemed just as baffled:

McGonagall's poetry with its execrable rhymes and fascination with contemporary disasters, continues to enjoy a bizarre popularity, and *Poetic Gems* has been republished many times.

Douglas Gifford does better in *The History of Scottish Literature*, but only after bemoaning 'the apparently unedifying situation' of McGonagall's enduring popularity compared to the more critically acclaimed contemporaries, Stevenson, James Thomson and John Davidson.

It is usually assumed that McGonagall is enjoyed because he is unintentionally amusing, and everyone likes a good laugh. True, if dubiously defensible. But we know from tested public performance, that an actor with a good voice can read the best of McGonagall (e.g. 'The Little Match Girl') quite straight and with some pathos. . . . If voice seems to be the key, we perhaps direct ourselves to Hamish Henderson's argument that the clumsy ametricality of the lines (on the page) can be related to McGonagall's Irish family background of 'come-all-ye' folk-song, the value of his poems being no more than that of their originality in uniquely and consistently forming their style out of the detritus of folk poetry. Perhaps anything carried to an extreme is attractive, as William Blake claimed.

McGonagall would have loved the sentiments even if the language in which they are couched is a mite mazy for a supposed elucidation. No matter, and how the poet and tragedian would have loved to have such luminaries as Hamish Henderson and William Blake rallied to his cause! Douglas Gifford has at least taken the trouble to read McGonagall even if he mis-read some of McGonagall's intentions.

There is the crucial observation about the work *in performance*, and he concludes, equally tellingly:

The obvious 'badness' of McGonagall also does not cancel the genuine popular appeal of someone who, unlike many of his contemporaries, gave himself the function of commenting on the noted public events of the time.

The thing that McGonagall got wrong was his own job description, 'poet and tragedian'. 'Tragedian and poet' would have served his case infinitely better. To drop another name into the fray which it seems, must forever attend his work, George Mackay Brown has said (to my wholehearted admiration and approval): 'There is no such thing as good poetry or bad poetry. There is only a poem, or a mess of words on the page.'

On that basis, William McGonagall wrote a handful of *poems*, including 'The Little Match Girl' and a marvellously touching little love poem of all things, 'Forget Me Not'. But the rest of his output is far from a mess of words on the page, for it is not poetry at all but scripts for the tragedian in him to perform. It was theatre, not poetry, which was his first love, and he had intellect enough to learn and perform Shakespeare as little more than a child. The fact that he *could* write his own individual and really moving poetry, but mostly chose not to, suggests he knew his market and knew exactly what he was doing. The greater body of his work resembles nothing so much as a cross between a town crier and a *Times* leader writer. His raw material was the great events of the day, and of history, the personalities of his era, and travelogues; the stuff, in other words, of journalism. But it was performance journalism, and the style of his performance was a degree of self-mockery which, he quickly discovered, paid better by far. His narratives, like 'The Execution of James Graham, Marquis of Montrose', and of course his greatest hits centring on the opening, the disaster and the rebuilding and reopening of the Tay Railway Bridge (solid gold to such a writer living in the very midst of such momentous international consternation) have a potent power in public performance which is quite absent on the printed page. So Gifford's assessment of him is right to conclude that voice is the key, but then he falls into the old critical trap of disdaining his 'clumsy ametricality'. It is not clumsy, but relaxed, and as such it increases the work's dramatic possibilities. McGonagall may have been vain, limited and gullible, but he was in control of his work. He was also courageous. It was not an easy way to make a living, to hire a space in a public house and then go out into the streets and drum up an audience for himself; to perform in an environment which (his own writings make quite plain) he loathed, be as much derided as applauded, then go out and do it the next night and the next. He was trained as a weaver and could have lived a much more ordered existence, but he was an actor at heart, a tragedian, a writer of his own scripts.

165

You do not, as Herr Wittig implied, need to be a psychiatrist to understand the popularity of William McGonagall, but it does help if you are a Dundonian. Dundee adopted him as enthusiastically as he adopted Dundee. He would not thank me for the comparison, but just as James McIntosh Patrick's prints adorn walls in Dundee which have never known another painting, so there are copies of McGonagall all over town in houses which would scorn a volume of Shakespeare or anything by any other poet who ever drew breath since. And all over Dundee this Christmas and next and the one after until God knows when, that slim book-shaped present poking a corner point into Christmas stockings from multis to mansions is one more copy of *Poetic Gems*. McGonagall's stock has probably never been higher and he could have prospered today on his royalties as he never did in his lifetime, and he would probably have a column in *The Sunday Post*.

I cannot remember how and when he first slipped into my consciousness, but I was certainly a child (and a devourer of books) and he was imbibed as effortlessly as Horlicks; as much a part of the fabric of my young Dundee life as football and Lyle's Golden Syrup and the Light Programme. As a child I did not rage at his 'clumsy ametricality' or despair that his rhymes were 'execrable'. I marvelled at him, at his ragged world of rhymes, that he wrote about Dundee and people with Dundee names like Gilfillan and Ballingall, places like Clepington and Baldovan and Magdalen Green and Monikie and Broughty Ferry, and he made you proud of Dundee – especially when he said one street of it meant more to him than all the sights of New York – and he made magic out of the Tay and turned it forever silvery.

An English teacher once raged at him and me because I wrote that I thought McGonagall's 'The Sorrows of the Blind' was a better poem than Milton's 'On His Blindness' (which was being thrust down our teenage throats at the time) because it spoke more directly and was more affecting. Memory is vague about the punishment, but it centred on writing far too many times to have any hope of being effective a line about the relative merits of Milton and McGonagall. To this day I find Milton an incomprehensible dust, but the silvery river keeps a perpetual flame burning in me for William Topaz McGonagall, poet and tragedian, sometime of this parish.

Chapter Fourteen

The Tay, The Tay

The tide is high, and slapping hard at the lifeboat shed. The river, full of urge and surge, is fast and at the end of the street. The seals which greeted the dawn from the broad uncovered beam of the sandbanks have torpedoed easily out and down into those deep elsewheres which are the habitat of the Tay's colony when the tide ushers them from the banks. Testily the swans stamp about their last hemmed-in yard of shingle shore, until they, too, take to the softer option of the waves and sit bouncing in the shallows beneath the harbour wall. The Ferry is never without seals and swans, and rarely without seal-watchers and swan-feeders. The swan herd grows in midwinter. Today it numbers twelve, eleven of them mute swans in various stages of maturity, from mud-brown first-year birds to a huge and dominant cob which defines the pecking order with an intimidating presence, the more intimidating (in this watcher's mind) because the brute force of which the bird is unquestionably capable is masked in gestures of such fluent grace. And there is a single whooper swan, Icelandic itinerant, conspicuously shyer than the mutes, but not as shy as he was when he arrived at the beginning of the week, learning to behave out of character in the interests of survival. The whooper's straight neck and vivid yellow and black wedge of a beak mark it out in the white throng. Seasoned swan-watchers know what it is. A few don't and conclude that there is something wrong with it: 'Eh'll be' it's ah they puhllutions in the wa'er . . . it's a deformi'y. Been sweemin owre near Dounreay or sompliss like tha.'

'Hingin mince, Wuhllie. It's a half-breed. It's a swan that's screwed a duck. It's a duck-billed swannypus.'

Swans are forever cropping up in my life and my writing. Theirs is the company I keep most gladly in all nature, addicted to their wild beauties and their sense of wild theatre, obsessed by their place in the mythology of all the world's continents; the same stories with the same details cropping up in the folklores of people of both hemispheres, stories of swans becoming people, people becoming swans. If you take on swans, you have much more than natural history to contend with.

I was here two days ago in the early evening, which is to say the darkness, standing on the river edge with the city and the bridges and the Fife shore reduced to their lights, headlands to their lighthouses, at the precise moment when the swan herd increased from ten to twelve. That little pier-end there where I stood gives a wider view of the Firth's unfathomable night blackness. The Tay is a mightier river by far at night. Amid the restless chatter and calling of gulls and waders, there came an unseen pulse of wings, like the sound of a child's humming-top broken into chords, a more urgent counter-pulse against the slow rhythm of waves. Measuring distance in darkness is an inexact science. I put the sound at perhaps two hundred yards, but it hove into sight at fifty, wing-striding upstream, then veering abruptly right into the mouth of the harbour. The pale blurs of two swans hardened to vivid whiteness, not, as I had imagined, twenty or thirty feet in the air, but cheating the wind down among the wavetops, so that as I stood on the pier they flew in below me and the harbour lights were on their backs, striking brilliance and shadows there as the wings beat. As I turned to follow their flight and their landing on the waves close to the herd, they unlocked an old memory of other swans emerging out of a different darkness. But it was a memory which, more telling than most in my nature-writer's life among swans, linked me forever – and gratefully – with this of all shores. I have written of that occasion before, in my 1992 book, *Waters of the Wild Swan*:

168

'I have been known to go to bizarre lengths to see swan spectacle at its utmost, pursuing a wildlife philosophy which is the antithesis of twitching. The twitcher travels to see a single bird once, to pronounce it seen. I travel to see that with which I am already intimately acquainted, but to see it again in a different light, to pronounce it seen more clearly or more profoundly, or just more. It was in such a spirit that I drove through one of the foulest days November can muster to a loch near the Buchan shore. At that time of year, the whoopers traditionally gather in their hundreds, six to seven hundred in a good year, and geese in five-figure hordes where the first of the five is not always a one.

'The height of the day's ambition was to see the biggest armada of swans of my life. Ten whoopers crossed my path a mile from the loch, which seemed to be a good omen but they proved to be the last swans I saw in flight until after dark. A dozen scattered desultorily about the loch itself, a dozen more mute swans kept them company. In the middle of the water there was a pack of coots so dense you could hardly see water through the mass. Counting them was hopelessly haphazard in the turgid light of noon flayed by sleety squalls on the sea wind. Twelve hundred was a reasonable assessment. The light began to fail about 3 p.m., and the day and the journey seemed doomed to dismal disappointment. But nature's saving graces rarely bypass patient vigils completely and no one with half an eye and a tolerable immunity to sitting and shivering it out through a few sodden grey and half-dark hours sees nothing. The vigil was attended first by a short-eared owl which came curious enough and close enough to fill the glasses, and directly overhead. A persistent wheezy monosyllable betrayed a young bird on a fence post fifty yards away and in the hour before the geese began to home in on the loch, there were four owls ghosting and stalling on some Buchan vole's last gasp.

'The first skein was a thousand strong and they came out of the north-west where the sky was palest, a shade of light black, the sound of them a fanfare such as a demented and hideously oversubscribed accordion band might perform. They wheeled in on a storm of wind-song, spilling air from their wings, whiffling down to a thousand giddy landings. The coot raft took to its heels at this, and sped over the surface in a solid stain to land three hundred yards away. They would shift twice more in the next half hour as the goose rain fell and fell, but settled eventually for the fact that so many geese in so little water left no hiding place. Soon there was little clear water to flee to so they simply sat blackly on and tholed the clamour as it grew and grew.

'The geese piled in, every few minutes a few hundred more — about twelve thousand pinkfeet in the space of an hour and a half, although those I missed as the light flew might have added two thousand more. It was the last of them, though, flying down the pitch darkness, which freed from time's snare a long-captive memory. It was a small skein and, unlike the rest, it came from the sea where the sky was almost coot-black and the birds invisible. I was aware first of a profound sense of dislocation, robbed not just of familiar landmarks but any landmarks at all, and in the worsening weather and the almost perversely solitary nature of the expedition, I felt suddenly and acutely alone. I clung, desperate for a consoling presence, to the haunting approach of the unseen geese down the night sky, my one familiar reference point. The sound, now that I isolated it in my mind from all the loch's wildfowl bustle, pitched me back thirty-five years to childhood winters on the edge of the Tay estuary. Suddenly, I was a seven-year-old, skidding on frosted pavements while walking home under the stars from Sunday tea at Aunty Meg's. The carol of the geese, the haloed sheen of gas streetlights, and my father's side were a trilogy of benevolent forces in which I delighted. For a few seconds by a lochside in Buchan, where I had never stood before and have not since, too cold and too alone for comfort, the wild geese spun me a chrysalis of childhood well-being.

'A deeper bugle sounded. The moment dispelled. The darkness offered up sixty-two whooper swans. I watched them land a dozen yards away and thrilled to them as I always do for their uncompromising wildness and their easy way with the far north of the world. I remembered then why I had come. If the journey in search of a swan armada could hardly be said to have achieved its purpose, I had made a richer discovery. It was the recognition that my own instinctive inclination towards the northlands of the world and their wild bird hordes was rooted in the rich seedbed of my own childhood; that my work now as a nature writer stemmed from the same root and was not, as I had so often uneasily imagined, a rootless acquisition. The continuity of Scottish tradition has always held profound significance for me, and suddenly I was aware of my own secure place in that tradition. It was a telling hour of my life. It all explained, too, my passion for whooper swans, and through them all swans, for the swans are merely variations on the same theme as the geese, and I simply crossed their path later in life. In the same moment, the nature writer's bond with nature was immeasurably strengthened.

'Sixty-two incoming whoopers, even in the dark, amount to a mighty consolation, and I left that shore finally satisfied that the spectacle is in the swan itself, that sixty or six hundred swans are no more perfect a creation than six swans, or one. It was a long way to go to discover such a simplistic truth.

'The darkness around me was suddenly full of wings, blacker than the night, frantic after the leisured ease of the swans' sudden appearance. It was the coots. They too had tholed enough of this water, and were leaving.'

Back in the bright noon of midwinter at the Ferry, my eye goes to the single whooper in the small white and wind-whetted maelstrom of the herd. Swans fascinate and baffle me more now than ever, and as if this jogging the memory of a memory wasn't enough confusion the memory that was jogged had long since grown thoroughly unsatisfactory as an explanation of my swan-love. The more I have scoured memory for the oldest associations with swans, the more I struggle with unsatisfactory theories which might account for the place of swans in my life and my work (that book; chapters in other books; a TV programme; two radio programmes; countless articles in newspapers; poems, an as-yet-unpublished novel; still more articles and photographs in magazines; thousands of hours in the field, watching them in every conceivable landscape arena from the Solway to Iceland, trying to fathom their secrets). Now, standing a few yards adrift from the small group of swan-feeders on the shore at the Ferry, my eye goes straight to the single whooper in the midst of the mutes and I watch nothing else as that packed swan-mass seethes. The other swans I see only as unfocused blurs which cross the path of my sightline to the whooper. He is quiet, aloof, reluctant, different, but urged by circumstance to scrap for this hand-out of winter sustenance, when he would rather not. He would rather be keeping the company of a small coterie of his own kind on some ocean-edge salt marsh or a peaty island lochan on Skye, or gorging among the stubbles and winter grasses and neep fields of the Carse of Stirling with the slow Forth or high, hidden moorland lochs nearby for safe roosting. He cannot stay, not like the mutes which will work this mile of peopled shore all winter. He is a traveller, a restless spirit, born on the circumference of the Arctic Circle, addicted to the ritual of winter migration between Iceland and Scotland, and even when he gets here he is thirled to a winter on the wing. He might go as far as Gloucestershire then cross to Norfolk, then north to Washington on the Tyne, west to Solway, north-east to the Carse of Stirling or Loch Leven, up the A9 to the Insh Marshes, north to the Black Isle, west to Skye, then, with spring on his wings, fly back up the ocean for a new nesting season in Iceland. But first, he must shake off the torpor of this hand-out herd. Perhaps he's injured, or a late arrival, or just resting between wherevers. His face and straight neck mark him out as different from the others, but only slightly different. He is clearly swan. But the real difference is inside him.

He pulls off to one side and sits watching on the water. I watch him watching. Then, in my ear, a voice:

'Jimmy! Ach yer no empethehsin wi swans again ur ye?' Alfie, newly cast-off from a lunchtime pint in The Ship.

'Whu' maks ye say that?

A bit too defensive that, for my own comfort.

Alfie points straight to the single whooper.

'Tha' ane, right?'

I shrugged.

'Look at it . . . look at you. It's standin awa fae the crowd. So ur you. It cannae keep awa fae the pliss whar it wis born. Same wi you. It cannae help itsel traivelin owre ah the pliss afore it turns an goes awa hame again. Wha dis tha remind you o, Jimmy? That whu' wiz goin on in yer heid?'

'It wisnae that organised, Alfie, but now you mention it . . .'

'Ken whu Eh think, Jimmy? Eh think you ur a swan, ane o they changelings yer aye writin aboo.'

'Alfie, that's a story. It's made up, right?'

'Either you're a swan, or its ah lehs you've been tellin iz fur ah they years.'

Alfie has the knack of delivering the most devastating piss-takes

I ever saw with the most dead-pan of faces. But when you've hung around him for a bit, and you've tuned in to his wavelength, you see the mischief in his eyes and I saw not a flicker of mischief. Then he did a thing he never did before, or since, just turned on his heel and walked. So I turned on mine, a few yards adrift from the small group of swan-feeders, and stared at the solitary whooper swan, a few yards adrift from the herd of mute swans, and I didn't much like what I had just heard.

And still I get further and further from what it is which keeps a flame burning in me for swans, nor why it should be that their neighbours in the Firth of Tay where I grew up, the seals out on the banks, are the only creatures with which (in the folklore of the northlands at least) man is willing to change places. It is a mixed blessing, a strain of Celtic blood in your dearest veins.

The Tay is all Dundee's saving graces. It is the par excellence ingredient in the city's setting. It is the source of benevolent light, that sea light harmonising much which would have rung discordant in a land-locked place. It softens Dundee's hard edges, permits enlightenment to infiltrate the mud-coloured walls, and puts the sound of curlews on our winter ears, which is never a bad thing. It is also the reason why Dundee exists, for all our eras of prosperity stemmed from our seagoing enterprise.

Today's Dundee docks are a profound disappointment to seagoing instincts, becalmed and cut off from the city, the majestic Customs House and the fearsomely armoured wooden frigate *Unicorn* marooned in undeserved solitary confinements. The great burnt umber gasholder with the 'sair heid' crown ('sair heids' were cakes that came in wrappers like bandages; they had a quarter of an inch of divine icing on top and they looked like pale gasholders, but they smelled better) . . . where was I? The gasholder glowers across Victoria Dock at the *Unicorn* which glowers in turn at the back of the Customs House. There was a time when the *Unicorn* was to keep the *Discovery* company, but Dundee as a city is still a newcomer to the tourism/heritage business, and there are times when a kind of amateurish indifference spikes good intentions and things get half done. So the *Discovery* sits in splendour with her own purpose-built domed temple, the prodigal daughter who came home, while the *Unicorn*, which has been our constant companion since 1873, gets a sandwich board, and tries to tempt you inside like an old whore. At the very least, she should have more promising surroundings, but if we are serious about our tourism/heritage, why should we preface anything with 'at the very least'? What's wrong with 'the very most' other than our own unfamiliarity with jumping into this most perplexing of businesses with both feet? So . . . a berth beside the *Discovery* and her three great masts and rigging restored so that she looks like the warmongering frigate she is and not a film-set stand-in for Noah's Ark. I know you can't make much of a play on words on *Unicorn* (William Topaz, where are you now that we need you?), but I am seeing six masts instead of three, two bowsprits instead of one, and two living legends of our ocean-going, lying cheek by jowl and ten times as potent a force for ourselves and our visitors as a hand-in-glove couple than in their present state of imposed and unamicable divorce.

For eight years through the 1980s, before I shed the journalistic yoke to write my books, I worked in Edinburgh and formed a passing attachment to the port of Leith. It appealed because it so reminded me of the Dundee I grew up in. Leith's shipping heyday is bygone, too, but it hasn't divorced itself from its waterfront. It has done the opposite. In these most difficult days for the seagoing places whose seagoing tides have ebbed, Leith has cemented the old marriage of town and dockland by building new houses in the docks and turning disused buildings (every harbour has them) into bars and restaurants, so Leithers are still accustomed to walking the docks for the hell of it, and water still cuts deep into the town centre, the way Dundee's used to. In that way, and until a new seagoing tide turns, old instincts are nurtured, the bond between firth and firth-dweller is kept supple as a good rope. It seems to me a matter of some urgency that Dundee finds a way to strengthen that old bond before it frays irretrievably. We must let the firth and its ships back in.

In the days when Shore Terrace meant what it said and accommodated the bus station, you could while away the wait between buses watching an endless succession of grubby rustbuckets – dredgers and other river workhorses – jostling and toiling on the other side of the street. When the no. 17 bus finally hove to alongside, you raced upstairs to improve the view of the dredger berthing or disgorging its holdful of sand into a patient queue of trucks. And that mysterious little species of railway engine was forever trundling along Dock Street and under the grotesque shadow of the Royal Arch, blackening its skirts with gleeful disrespect. It was an everyday occurrence for your bus to have to overtake a train in Dock Street.

Occasionally, a lightship would be hauled in for repainting or refitting, or to have its bulb changed (as we bairns used to joke among ourselves). The lightship was as exotic as Dundee's street-parking boats could muster, a vivid red peacock among so many sparrows, but it was all a part of our lives, part of workaday Dundee, part of the pattern of our sea-smelling streets. To this day, more than thirty years after we had it removed from our midst to accommodate the road bridge, we still miss it.

You still see old folk trying to get to the waterfront from what's left of Shore Terrace and Dock Street. They walk the old routes like Aborigines pursuing Songlines. They are mindful of the day when Union Street pointed at the Fifies (the Tay Ferries terminal; Dundee never called them anything but Fifies), fearful of the boxed-in corridors; scornful of the regime which planted acres of roads and no pavements here. So they take all manner of risks, towing grandchildren to the wrong side of barriers meant to keep them out, pausing amid the oblivious press of traffic by the shrubbery of a roundabout. And all because wandering down to the docks is what they have always done. Nothing could be more natural to a Dundee laddie of any age at all than to stroll along a quayside watching the business of ships. It's just that it shouldn't be so difficult.

I miss the Fifies more than the rest of it, for while the dredgers, coasters, lightships and the others were the exclusive preserve of the mysterious cabal of seamen with their own language and seafaring rituals, the Fifies were boats at our disposal. They were big and broad-beamed and open-decked. They smelled of seaweed and diesel. They reminded me of elephants. They caressed the wooden piers when they berthed with all the maternal douceness of a cow elephant nuzzling a new calf. Then they turned into the open firth and charged the waves and head-butted the squalls like a rogue bull. Always they were elephants, just as mighty, just as tender, just as otherworldly; magical passports to Newport and the low, green world

175

of Fife. Fifers were different. They talked differently. They didn't live in cities, but in rows of low-to-the-ground cottages with pantiled roofs. They kept dogs and racing pigeons and they looked across the water at Dundee and shuddered at its immense greyness. But they came over on Saturdays to shop or go to the match, or on Sundays to visit relatives and stay for tea. We had this in common with them: they loved the Fifies too.

What the Fifies did for you was let you dawdle out in midstream, let you become a moving fragment of the Tay itself, let you eyeball the dredgers as they heaved and gouged at the sandbanks, let you lean out over the bow and wave at seals, let you cut your own swathe across the silvery Tay. And at any point in the voyage, you could turn to face the stern and look back at Dundee on its twa hulls through a gauze of gulls as it folded back into its Angus landscape and you knew in your heart why some folk call it bonnie. On the return voyage, Dundee was all you had eyes for. It grew and grew and the Ahld Steeplie hardened in its midst, and the place opened its embrace and welcomed you home. The Fifie berthed, and like the good elephant she was, she put you down gently and you liked to pat her great flank as you stepped ashore. Post Office picnics to Windmill Park, summer days in the seeven weekies to the Braes at Newport or the beach at Tayport, bike runs to Balmerino, car runs to Uncle Bert's at Springfield (and always a dash through the darkening fields to catch the last boat). No trip on the Fifies ever had a drab purpose or a disappointing destination, and not the least of it all was that at the end of the day, there was always the Fifie home.

No bridge ever did that for you. There was a day in the early 1960s, when the first temporary bridge phase of the road bridge construction was more or less complete and the *Scotscraig*'s engines failed in midstream, and quite out of control (rogue elephant to the last) she slipped into the downstream current and charged the bridge. And when she rammed it at the speed of the river, there were plenty of Dundee stalwarts who said it was an omen, and not a few who wandered down to the docks and cheered her when she was towed home. McGonagall would surely have made something of that, as he rarely passed up an opportunity to pontificate a poem on the silvery business of the Tay, her bridges, and her maritime misfortunes.

Relax! Just as, when I wrote my book, *Among Islands*, I pledged

that it would contain no quotation from Boswell and Johnson, I have
pledged also that this will be a Dundee book with no parody of a
McGonagall poem. It is enough that I have already written a speech
for him. Besides, why mock when the original is unsurpassable? The
silvery Tay served his muse well, and he was the river's most devoted
publicist. Not only did two railway bridges and the disaster which
befell the first:

'On the last Sabbath day of 1879
Which will be remember'd for a very long time'

coincide with the height of his powers, and provide him with his
greatest hits, but his dramatic instincts and his journalistic nose for a
story were just as tellingly roused when on . . . what was that date
again, William Topaz McGonagall? You were there after all.

'Twas in the month of December, and in the year 1883.'

Yes, thank you. Well, go on man, go on . . .

That a monster whale came to Dundee,
Resolved for a few days to sport and play,
And devour the small fishes in the silvery Tay.

Ah, the famous Tay Whale! To me it was never anything more than
a skeleton suspended from a Dundee museum ceiling, a tormentor of
childhood dreams. But you were there, William Topaz. How did the
local people react when the news broke?

When it came to be known a whale was seen in the Tay,
Some men began to talk and to say,
We must try and catch this monster of a whale,
So come on, brave boys, and never say fail.

Then the people together in crowds did run,
Resolved to capture the whale and to have some fun!
So small boats were launched on the silvery Tay,
While the monster of the deep did sport and play.

So how did the whale take to all this?

177

Oh! It was a most fearful and beautiful sight,
To see it lashing the water with its tail all its might,
And making the water ascend like a shower of hail,
With one lash of its ugly and mighty tail.

I'm not too sure about your simile there, William Topaz. Surely a shower of hail *de*-scends?

Then the water did descend on the men in the boats

Right. You were stringing me along. So what was the effect of all that water on the men in the boats?

Which wet their trousers and also their coats;
But it only made them more determined to catch the whale,
But the whale shook at them his tail.

So they're soaked but determined? When do we get to the bit about the harpoons? That's going to be a tricky rhyme for you?

And they laughed and grinned just like wild baboons,
While they fired at him their sharp harpoons:
But when struck with the harpoons he dived below,
Which filled his pursuers' hearts with woe:

Woe?! Why woe?

Because they guessed they had lost a prize,
Which caused the tears to well up in their eyes;
And in that their anticipations were only right,
Because he sped on to Stonehaven with all his might:

Stonehaven? Why the hell did it go to Stonehaven? Oh, never mind. What happened next? It couldn't have got as far as Stonehaven without being spotted?

And was first seen by the crew of a Gourdon fishing-boat

Thought so. What did they make of it?

> Which they thought was a big coble upturned afloat;
> But when they drew near they saw it was a whale,
> So they resolved to tow it ashore without fail.

Tow it ashore? A monster whale – your very words, William Topaz, and they are going to *tow* it ashore with a fishing-boat? How do they plan to do that, given that it sped here with all its might?

> So they got a rope from each boat tied round its tail
> And landed their burden at Stonehaven without fail;
> And wh . . .

Hold it, hold it! This is the tail that lashed the water and almost drowned the Dundee lads in their boat. Now it lies still in the water while the Stonehaven chiels slip a noose round it?

Listen. I'm a poet and tragedian. Not a bloody engineer. Do you want the rest of the story or not?

Okay, okay, what's your overview of the whole drama? Why did a whale turn up here in the first place?

> And my opinion is that God sent the whale in time of need,
> No matter what other people may think or what is their creed;
> I know fishermen in general are often very poor,
> And God in His goodness sent it to drive poverty from their door.

Yep. That would explain it. So they cut up the carcase and it fed them right through the winter?

> So Mr John Wood has bought it fo . . .

Bought it! You mean they sold the bloody thing? The people of Stonehaven sold a dead whale? What did they get for it? A fiver a ton?

Look, I'm on the second last verse.

Pray be silent or I'll kick your erse. Now look what you've made me do. That's a McGonagall parody you've made me write. To conclude:

So Mr John Wood has bought it for two hundred and twenty-six pound
And has brought it to Dundee all safe and all sound;
Which measures forty feet in length from the snout to the tail,
So I advise the people far and near to see it without fail.

Then hurrah! for the mighty monster whale,
Which has got seventeen feet, four inches from tip to tip of a tail!
Which can be seen for a sixpence or a shilling,
That is to say, if the people all are willing.

Thank you William Topaz McGonagall.
My pleasure, Sir, your humble servant.

Chapter Fifteen

Eh'll Tak Yer Pho'ie

The box is wide and shallow and grey. It probably contained a dress when it was delivered. It has my mother's name and address handwritten on it, and the logo of D.M. Brown's, 'The Store That Satisfies'. Satisfied, actually, for D.M.'s is long gone, consumed by some chain or other, those chains which devour High Street individuality and independence and replace them with lower common denominators. Dundee lost not just D.M.'s but also G.L.'s, Smith Brothers and Draffens, focal points of my mother's coterie of friends every Saturday morning, memorable to my childhood eyes for school trenchcoats, tearooms, and Toylands, not necessarily in that order. All of which has nothing to do with the box.

It is not the first box, but boxes which are used to store the family archive of old photographs, and which are forever being slid in and out from under the bed, are bound to burst about the seams from time to time. This is the second box I can remember, and its stout cardboard is beginning to rupture. There are not just photographs here. There are Dad's retirement cards, a couple of sympathy cards and letters to Mum when Dad died in 1975, poignant scraps of Dad's military career, and (inexplicably) a guide to Norwich Cathedral.

It is, like any family archive, not an archive at all, but a thoroughly unmethodical and haphazard repository. Its oldest photograph was taken perhaps a hundred years ago, and others have been removed at every intervening era to be processed in a more orderly existence in photograph albums. Occasions and identities are unannotated. The photographs are unsorted, and every time the box is moved, generations shift and tumble among unaccustomed bedfellows and time falls head over its own heels. My eighteen-year-old self, guitar in hand, might spill between aunts and find myself coming to rest against my father's army truck. Or my mother, sixty and still glamorous in a spectacular blue wedding outfit, might startle at the sight of her teenage self in a short-skirted chorus line of wolf-whistleable dancers.

The oldest photograph was a mystery. It's a formal turn-of-the-century portrait cut and mounted in a manner which suggests it once occupied an oval frame (silver and in a drawing-room as my mind's eye sees it, though few enough if any of our copious forebears were in the drawing-room class). It is of a woman, perhaps in her thirties, the face powerful rather than pretty, forbidding almost. The eyes are heavy-lidded, unsmiling, unfathomable, the mouth wide and possibly a touch crooked, although that could be the consequence of the primitive nature of the camera. Only one side of the face and the dress is sharp. The chin is square and looks as if it might belong to my father's family rather than my mother's, but it doesn't. There is nothing of Dad's family (other than the famous goalkeeper pictures, and they were never part of the box's population) until he appears himself as a young man. No, the mystery portrait was almost certainly a maternal forebear, although she resembles no one so much as a young and slightly softened-up Rikki Fulton in drag. I guessed at an aunt, great-aunt or grandmother of my mother's, possibly her Aunt Nellie, who died before Mum was born, the Nellie whose name she was saddled with to her lifelong chagrin. Mind you, that same mother of mine tried to persuade me to call my first daughter Hauldean, her mother's name, but mercifully my wife Val and I had already decided to call her after no one, so she's Morag and (I hope) grateful for my resolve in the face of my mother's heavily dropped hints.

A snapshot of memory suddenly crystallises all of this. Morag was still a child and we were on a family visit to Mum's house in the Ferry. Morag had befriended a neighbour's child there, and when she went outside clutching a new toy camera, the Dundee child greeted her with: 'Morag! Eh'll tak yer pho'ie.' I should explain that my children have been brought up, not in Dundee, but in Stirling, and this excited outburst of raw Dundee fell as incomprehensibly on Morag's ears as Yiddish. She turned helplessly to us for translation, and when my mother had wiped away the last of her tears of laughter, she turned to me very quietly and seriously and said: 'You must alway keep photographs.'

She belonged to that species and generation of Dundee folk who gathered old photographs assiduously and pored over them often, regurgitating the same old stories so often that I am as familiar with some of them as she was when she lived through them, and doubtless that was her intention. But the remorseless exposure to mild embarrassment which was my enduring emotion each time the box was exhumed has left me with a quiet distaste for boxes of old photographs. Partly, too, that state of affairs has been accounted for by her insistence on adding to the store of photographs at every opportunity, despite a certain instinctive photographic ineptitude. Thus the box (and the albums and sundry unsorted folders of prints) contains any number of overexposed thoughtlessly composed pictures of people without feet standing under acres of sky. But the occasions are recorded, after a fashion, and although, of course, she was right to urge me to keep photographs, I never have, and when I get a camera out it is to point it at a mountain or a swan, and the role of family archivist falls to others.

I went in search of the mystery woman's identity by consulting the only oracle I could think of, my mother's brother, Stuart Illingworth, a vigorous eighty-something, and his wife, Helen. So I drove over the hill to the Perthshire village of Forteviot, to the house with the warmest welcome I know. Wherever they have called home – Edinburgh, Peebles and Perth before Forteviot – and for all of my life, more or less, I have been accustomed to the idea of visiting them, and never contemplated the idea with anything other than enthusiasm. Stuart Illingworth gave me my first bird book, taught me to use my first camera, gave me my first malt whisky, advised me on the political wisdom of Scottish Nationalism, towed my brother and me around the countryside on bike runs (he still cycles twenty-mile runs 'on good days') and, apart from my father, he had as much influence on my young life as any man I can think of.

The picture was easy. 'That's your great-grandmother. She was a right little tyrant, too. My grandfather was about six foot three and she was about five foot one. And the very devil.'

'What was her name?'

'Well, Barrie, but her first name . . . no, I've no idea.'

So I looked at the face I had puzzled over with new respect, and despite my uncle's disparaging character reference, it is no small significance to unearth a photograph of my great-grandmother, even if she was a witch. I looked long and hard at the face and I could find no shred of resemblance to any other relative I ever encountered. But there she was, and she had a swan at her throat.

I put another picture from the box's obscure hoard in front of my uncle, a group of three young men and three young women, who for reasons best known to themselves had swopped hats for the pose, the women wearing the men's bowlers, the men wearing the women's more ornate hats. All of them have studied po-faced expressions which hint at tightly suppressed mirth. *Something* is going on.

'That's your grandfather, and that's your grandmother.' My uncle pointed to the two on the end of the group, both of them so young that again I could fathom no hint of the old man and woman who survive among my earliest childhood memories.

'It may even have been before they were married.' That puts the photograph in the first few years of the century. It is quite likely that the most po-faced of the group, my grandmother, the same Hauldean Barrie, was one of the ringleaders of whatever high jinks are being just about contained. She was, as my mother confirmed often, an unfulfilled actress with a beautiful singing voice and a passion for the stage. All of that explains why she insisted on elocution for her children, and the photograph which shows her on stage in front of a soft focus countryside set, portraying (it must be said) not the prettiest fairy you ever saw, but unquestionably a fairy. The barely faded pencil inscription on the back is 'Love from Fairy Illingworth'.

Mum swallowed her mother's inclinations whole, and the box coughs up two cameos of her young stage 'career', one a Bo-Peepish figure in a blonde wig, the other a mini-skirted teenage dancer in a chorus line of six.

There is even a certain theatricality about a rough-edged and creased snap of Mum aged about six with both her brothers, Stuart and Eric. Mum and Eric are in a kind of prototype piler, an open box on discarded pram wheels, while their older brother stands behind. Mum wears a cape with a hood, Eric a velvet jacket with a frilly collar and a Flower-Pot Man hat, which was hardly everyday wear in the streets of Lochee for 1920s bairns. Mum hated the hood. I remember her anguish recalling how 'the boys' used to follow her shouting 'Little Red Riding Hood' at her. It seems a mild enough taunt compared to what might be flung after a lassie in a cape and hood in Lochee now, and as for a laddie in a frilly collar . . .

As for the 'vehicle':

'I remember that! It was a cartie my father made for us,' Stuart told me. I thought I recognised the style of the designer, for the hand was that of the same Bill Illingworth who, thirty years or so later, built all manner of wooden toys for my brother and me.

There is nothing of my father's childhood in the box. He emerges in its unscripted story fully fledged and a soldier. The most affecting relic of his service life is his Soldier's Service and Pay Book in its brown-cloth cover, its heavy official type and its period piece language:

ALL RANKS

REMEMBER – Never discuss military, naval or air matters in public or with any stranger, no matter to what nationality he may belong.

The enemy wants information about you, your unit, your destination. He will do his utmost to discover it.

Keep him in the dark. Gossip on military subjects is highly dangerous to the country, whereas secrecy leads to success.

BE ON YOUR GUARD and report any suspicious individual.

I don't know what I expected of a Soldier's Service and Pay Book. I did not even know such a thing existed, far less that I would stumble upon my father's in the box, fifty years after he last had any use for it. The troubled and penurious nature of his young life was somehow implicit in the blandness of the information and a certain amount of defacing among his personal details:

Number, name, date of birth, place of birth (this entry heavily obliterated by a later hand than the green ink of the original), trade on enlistment (given as 'grocer' which probably amounted to delivering groceries by bike or cart), nationality of father at birth, nationality of mother at birth (these two were likewise obliterated by the same blue-black determination), religious denomination, enlisted at Perth on 12 January 1932 for the Regular Army – three years with the Colours and nine in the Reserve. He was nineteen. His physical description was startling – '5ft 7¾", 150 lbs, maximum chest 34"', a rake. Under 'Next of Kin' after blank sections opposite 'Wife' (he was unmarried then), 'Children', 'Father' (that old wound), 'Mother' (she had died in 1918), 'Brothers or Sisters' (he had five), the only entry is under 'Other Relations': 'Aunt, Miss Margaret Anderson' – Auntie Meg.

The ugly bruise of the heavy-handed deletions can only have been done after demob in 1945. Alterations of that nature were strictly forbidden in the list headed 'Instructions to Soldier'.

I wish now that I could penetrate that mind then which tried to expunge that one official acknowledgement of his parents' existence from the record of his life, even after the document it so besmirched had ceased to have any validity other than as a souvenir of that military way of life and that war. That other conflict he carried in his mind for the rest of his days. A better wish: I wish now that I could be reassured of his peace of mind.

THE UNERECTED STONE
Did you leave your mortal mind
behind deep in the dark earth
to moulder softly, decomposing
all its old accumulated pains?

Did you travel to your hereafter,
wherever, kitted out with a clean sheet?
Have you grasped the Goalie's hand
and clasped your mother close yet?

And made your peace?

Do you see now what was blind,

186

left behind for me to ponder
over a cold and unerected stone?
Did you becalm that storm you took
to your untranquil grave?

And do you see well why the hell
you had to die so young?

Among the other military souvenirs in the box is a regimental
Christmas card for 1943 with the message 'With best wishes for a
happy Christmas and a victorious New Year' printed in gothic script
and the handwritten message to my mother underneath: 'All my love,
Jim'. The other side is emblazoned with a Desert Rat and the now
famous names of the Eighth Army's campaign thus far . . . El
Alamein . . . Tunis . . . Tripoli, these three picked out in capital letters
from a list of seventeen. And there is the programme for the British
Victory Parade in Berlin, 21 July 1945.

And now that it has only recently come to light, my brother and
I can add to the box's store the briefest of notes from my father to
Auntie Meg: 'Back safe. Hope to see you soon.' Its arrival was
announced by the postie bellowing up the stairs: 'Your laddie's safe!'

With that message, Auntie Meg learned for the first time that Dad
had made it safely back to Britain from Dunkirk. It may have been a
bastard of a war, but for my father, it was never dull.

There are also the photographs: Dad beside his truck (he was
trained as a driver and mechanic) and being in the Royal Horse
Artillery; there is Dad with his horse, Mary's Lamb, which he cursed
roundly and affectionately for evermore. It had been named by a
sadist, but for the rest of his life he never passed a horse in a field
without stopping to greet it and slip it a furtive Polo mint. I think I
have seen him do that in almost every county in Scotland. There is
Dad in the desert, Dad in uniform (including one preposterously
young and coy on which he has scribbled to Mum, 'Are you laughing
at this?' Probably.). There is Dad in his demob suit. It must be his
demob suit because it is quite the worst piece of cloth I have ever
seen on him. It fits where it touches, it looks as if he had slept in it,
and it looks as if it was made for a fifty-four-inch chest rather than a
thirty-four. The tie is about a foot long and protruding from the

jacket. But the breadth of his smile is one I recognise. For the rest of his life, Dad had his suits handmade and dressed with quiet and dark impeccability.

The smallest photograph in the box is a faded sepia snap of Dad in uniform, open necked, standing at ease, smiling, and it is cut into an oval. For as long as I can remember, it was in a silver oval locket which my mother wore often. It had been her mother's, and it is now my daughter Morag's. Mum insisted she should have it in time because once when she was very young, Morag bit the locket while Mum was wearing it and left the imprint of one of her first teeth there. So a new thread of continuity is woven into the fabric of the box's story, and an old silver locket has a new story to tell, now that it has survived its longest era of peace.

With Dad home from the war it was hardly surprising that 1946 coughed up my brother, Vic, although Mum at least was surprised (to put it mildly) when 1947 coughed up me. As she put it with her customary absence of tact: 'When I knew I was expecting you, I nearly drowned myself.' I arrived anyway and Vic and I make our début in the box aged about three and two in Lochee High Street, Mum pushing me in a prototype species of buggy, Dad leading Vic by the hand. It is a street photographer's picture, snatched without permission and then sold after my parents had been told they had just had their photgraphs taken; a dangerous way to make a living, I would guess. As it is, he had concentrated wholly on Mum, she being the pretty one of the four, and cut off Dad's left ear and left shoulder. Still, you get the gist of a healthy young family out for a summer stroll, although why we were strolling Lochee High Street, I can't imagine. It must also be said, to be kind about it, that neither Vic nor I look undernourished, although ration books were still a part of a young mother's weekly shopping ritual.

Ration books! It is an all but incomprehensible idea now, we who think nothing of heaping a Ben Nevis of food on to a supermarket trolley because the shops close for a day at New Year. Even then, by the time they lodged in my mind, they were on the way out. Where I remember them – or fancy I remember them, for I could have been no more than four – was in my mother's old leather shopping-bag in Glamis Road's only shop, a timber shack standing on a square of cinders on the edge of the farm. (Farmland flowed from the other side of the street clear across to the Sidlaws, a benevolent sea for a young child until tides of bungalows and council schemes like Menzieshill obliterated it. In the days of the shack-shop, Menzies Hill was just a hill with a sublime view of the Tay.) Long before I was tall enough to see over the counter, the shop was flattened to make way for a new three-shop unit, and the farm's days were numbered. Mind you, it was a coarse and filthy farm inhabited by an uncouth tribe of boys with arseless breeks who swore and threw stones instead of saying hello. But it had a stackyard, and barn owls ghosted among the haystacks for mice and rats, and their voice was as much a part of winter nights as overhead geese.

So what I remember of that frontier shop was the front of the counter. It was faced with a peculiar surface of small round bulges like half-sunk Maltesers. My chubby fingers preoccupied themselves at every visit with trying to prise one free, for I was certain they were sweeties.

The three shops which rose where the shack fell were a newsagent, a butcher, and Andrew G. Kidd's, Dundee baker of legend. Kidd's was paradise, because it smelled of new baking and introduced my childhood and its teeth to boilings. The butcher's arrival did not prevent our household from continuing to patronise Baird's in Lochee, which had always served us with a quality of good-humoured courtesy and which from this distance of time feels like an all but extinct period piece. The three-mile round-trip was always deemed worth the effort.

But now that I care to think about it, such courtesy was part of our lives. Both my parents were strict on good manners. We were taught early to give up our seat on a crowded bus, and learned much more, unbidden, by their example. That courtesy was returned by endless callers at the prefab – the rent man, the insurance man, the coalie, the lemonade man, the icey, the man from the store delivering the weekly order of groceries. The words 'store' and 'order' only had one meaning in my young life. The Store was the S.C.W.S. in Lochee and the order was what they delivered. I used to help Mum to compile the list which she then phoned, quoting her divi number – 9049. What rubbish the memory's store delivers to order.

Back in the box, I have discovered wheels – sharing a pedal car with my brother and (a masterpiece among the box's random art) exploring among the high fields of Elmwood Road on my trike. The trike has only two mudguards. Being mine, it would have. I have obviously been dressed for the occasion by my mother for the scarf is appallingly neat and I am wearing (the shame!) a cap. I must be six, and I daresay it was the last hat I owned. A young friend, Davie Bruce, frowns desperately on a miniature two-wheeler, as well he might. My younger daughter, Heather, confronted with the picture for the first time, said:

'Is that Dad? He looks like Oor Wullie.'

I choose to take that as the highest of compliments.

The box recalls how Vic and I begin to grow tall and slim and different. I begin to appear in open-necked and sleeves-up shirts. Vic gets collar-and-tie smart. Mum and Dad grow handsomely middle-aged. Suddenly, I have become eighteen, posing with that white guitar which felled the drunken bride at her wedding up the Blahcky; the thinking man's Bert Weedon.

The one photo in the whole box I really like shows the four of us outside the flat, leaning on the boot of Dad's Cortina, casual, relaxed, happy, healthy, apparently pleased with each other's company. Vic was a student by then and I was an embryonic journalist. We were both about to step across the threshold in directions of our own, but at the moment, skylarks and kestrels and owls haunted the field and the Hully at our back door, and life was as good as it looked. Dundee, you were bonnie then.

No, here is one more photograph I like. It is of my mother, attending a wedding some time after Dad died. She dredged up every scrap of her prodigious faith – her 'rock', she called it – to deal with Dad's death from cancer at sixty-three, and her reserves of courage and stamina and natural optimism never failed her. She is a merry widow all in blue in the photograph, and as pretty and smiling as ever. From those very youngest stage-struck photographs, her face hardly changed at all. The only time I vividly recall her face looking as if it had forgotten how to smile and be pretty, she was in bed in King's Cross Hospital and she had been dead for just one hour.

The lid of the box is burst at one corner, so it slips back on more easily than it used to. It will be a while before I open it again.

NELLIE (An unpainted portrait of my mother)

Pastel framed in ebony.
Form classical.
Perspectives sure, not always
terminated by logic.
Texture unroughened
by age or death.
Song, laugh, wit,
clear-eyed grit
the artist caught; he missed
the understones of faith
and giving (their depths
were infinite – you can't
paint that).

He also missed
a light she'd lit
within. I think
my father saw it.
I saw some good things
by its radiance.